Growing Up Is Hard to Do

A collection of *Booklist* Columns

Edited by Sally Estes

BOOKLIST Publications
American Library Association
1994

Designed by Stuart Whitwell

ISBN: 0-8389-7726-X

Contents

Introduction

This compilation of 12 retrospective bibliographies previously published in *Booklist* can serve as a popular-reading companion to *Genre Favorites for Young Adults: A Collection of Booklist* Columns, published by *Booklist* Publications in 1993. Though geared primarily to the junior- and senior-high-school-age reader, the collection also contains titles that will appeal to upper-level middle-schoolers.

The lists have been updated and expanded; some have been adapted from bibliographies that appeared in the Books for Young Adults section before it was merged with the Children's Books section to become Books for Youth in September 1990. For example, "Growing Up during World War II" was published in *Booklist* as "The Blitz to the Bomb: WWII Fiction" in 1988; here, the emphasis is on growing up, and war stories that do not convey the effect of the war on young people have been omitted.

Adult fiction and nonfiction with appeal for YAs as well as titles written specifically for young people appear on all the lists, offering a wide range of titles for a variety of reading tastes and maturity levels. All titles have been checked against the current *Books in Print,* and paperback editions have been added when available. The compilation also includes "Growing Up Listening," a list of audiobooks that may attract non- and reluctant readers or may simply expand the literary experience for teenage readers/listners.

The many bibliographies about growing up in various ethnic groups, which have been used in Hazel Rochman's *Against Borders: Promoting Books for a Multicultural World* (*Booklist* Publications/ALA Books 1993), are not included here.

Sally Estes
Editor, Books for Youth
Booklist

Growing Up Female

Selected by Books for Youth associate editor Stephanie Zvirin and assistant editor Hazel Rochman, the following bibliography celebrates womanhood and coming of age. Including fact and fiction, classic and contemporary titles, it reflects the anguish confusion, passion, and joy of growing up female. The list introduces a wide range of concerns—from overcoming poverty and prejudice and making decisions about work and sex, to breaking away from one's parents or choosing to stay home.

Angelou, Maya. I Know Why the Caged Bird Sings. 1970. Random, $21 (0-394-42986-9); Bantam, paper, $4.99 (0-553-27937-8).

Gr. 9–12. Candid and poetic, the first of Angelou's autobiographical accounts describes her growing up black in the South.

Ansa, Tina M. Baby of the Family. 1989. Harcourt, $18.95 (0-15-110431-X).

Gr. 9–12. Steeped in the black culture of 1950s rural Georgia, this is the affecting, loving, and often humorous coming-of-age story of Lena, a "special" child born with a caul and the ability to see ghosts and predict the future.

Arrick, Fran. Steffie Can't Come Out to Play. 1978. Bradbury, o.p.; Dell, paper, $2.50 (0-440-97635-9).

Gr. 9–12. Fourteen-year-old Stephanie runs away from her unhappy home to New York City, where she's lured into prostitution by a clever pimp from whom she cannot seem to break away.

Atwood, Margaret. Cat's Eye. 1989. Doubleday, $18.95 (0-385-26007-5); Bantam, paper, $5.95 (0-553-38247-6).

Gr. 9–12. Atwood's candid, witty, and intensely moving novel about a feminist artist who remembers growing up in the 1940s and 1950s evokes the vicious, ob-

sessive power games among young girls who are "friends."

Auel, Jean. Clan of the Cave Bear. 1980. Crown, $19.95 (0-517-54202-1); Bantam, paper, $6.99 (0-553-25042-6).

Gr. 9–12. An orphaned Cro-Magnon child, adopted into a clan of Neanderthal hunter-gatherers, grows into womanhood and into a gradual awareness that her survival is linked to that of humankind.

Austen, Jane. Pride and Prejudice. 1813. Numerous hardbound and paper editions available.

Gr. 8–12. In a witty nineteenth-century comedy of manners, the five Bennett daughters, prodded by their ambitious mama, confront "society" in search of husbands and happiness.

Benoit, Joan and **Baker, Sally.** Running Tide. 1987. Knopf, $16.95 (0-394-55457-4).

Gr. 9–12. After breaking a leg in high school while training for ski competition, Benoit turned to running and went on to win a gold medal in the 1984 Olympic marathon race.

Boissard, Janine. A Matter of Feeling. 1980. Little, Brown, o.p.; Fawcett, paper, $2.50 (0-449-70213-8).

Gr. 9–12. Seventeen-year-old budding writer Pauline Moreau, the third of four daughters, tells how her warm French family sustains her through her passionate first love for an older artist.

Bond, Nancy. A Place to Come Back To. 1984. Macmillan/Margaret K. McElderry, $15.95 (0-689-50302-4).

Gr. 7–10. Charlotte has been friends with Oliver since childhood, but now their relationship is changing. She knows that he loves her and that he needs her desperately, but it's hard for them to reach out to each other.

Bridgers, Sue Ellen. Home before Dark. 1976. Knopf, $13.99 (0-394-93299-4); Bantam, paper, $2.50 (0-553-26432-X).

Gr. 7–10. When her father abandons the life of a migratory worker to settle in a sharecropper's cabin on his brother's tobacco farm, Stella Mae comes to realize that she needs human more than material roots.

Brontë, Charlotte. Jane Eyre. 1847. Numerous hardbound and paper editions available.

Gr. 8–12. Orphaned and abused as a child, Jane grows up fighting to believe in herself, and working as a governess in a great house, she falls in love with the brooding, passionate master, Mr. Rochester.

Brooks, Bruce. Midnight Hour Encores. 1986. HarperCollins, $14 (0-06-020709-4); paper, $3.95 (0-06-447021-0).

Gr. 7–12. Eighteen-year-old cellist prodigy Sib feels she's done it all herself, until, on a journey to find her mother, she discovers her father's strength and his need.

Cheong, Fiona. The Scent of the Gods. 1991. Norton, $19.95 (0-393-03024-5); paper, $8.95 (0-393-31012-4).

Gr. 9–12. This haunting coming-of-age story evokes a turbulent 1960s Singapore through the eyes of orphaned 11-year-old Su Yen, who is being reared by a grandmother trying to preserve the traditional Chinese way of life.

Coman, Carolyn. Tell Me Everything. 1993. Farrar, $15 (0-374-37390-6).

Gr. 6–9. Feeling betrayed, adrift, and, at times, guilty, 12-year-old Roz is driven to discover what really happened on the mountain when her mother fell to her death, and in trying to put the past behind her, Roz embarks, instead, on a journey of self-discovery.

Cooney, Caroline B. Don't Blame the Music. 1986. Putnam, $14.95 (0-448-47778-5).

Gr. 8–12. Susan's comfortable, satisfying life topples when older sister Ashley returns home, bringing hate, bitterness, and a madness that affects the whole family and shakes Susan out of her complacency.

Cross, Gillian. Chartbreaker. 1987. Holiday, $14.95 (0-8234-0647-4); Dell, paper, $2.95 (0-440-20312-0).

Gr. 8–12. Vulnerable and ugly, teenage rock star Finch sings "like concentrated danger," her performance charged with rage and with her love for the band leader, Christy.

Daly, Maureen. Seventeenth Summer. 1942. Dodd, o.p.; Pocket/Archway, paper, $2.95 (0-671-61931-4).

Gr. 7–12. A small Wisconsin town is the background for a story that transcends its 1940s aura in its depiction of the angst and awe of a teenage girl's first love.

Dillard, Annie. An American Childhood. 1987. HarperCollins, paper, $11 (0-06-091518-8).

Gr. 9–12. "I grew up in Pittsburgh in the 1950s in a house full of comedians, reading books," states Dillard in an affectionate, witty, episodic celebration of her childhood and family.

Dorris, Michael. A Yellow Raft in Blue Water. 1987. Holt, $16.95 (0-8050-0045-3); Warner, paper, $9.99 (0-446-38787-8).

Gr. 9–12. In a tale of three generations, 15-year-old half-Indian Rayona longs for a cozy suburban family, but her mother abandons her on the barren Montana reservation with her fierce grandmother, who doesn't know her and doesn't want to.

Emecheta, Buchi. The Bride Price. 1976. Braziller, paper, $7.95 (0-8076-0951-X).

Gr. 9–12. The tragic story of a modern Nigerian girl, Akunna, who rebels against traditional marriage customs and elopes with the schoolmaster she loves.

Fathers: Reflections by Daughters. Ed. by Ursula Owen. 1985. Pantheon, $17.95 (0-394-53913-3); paper, $7.95 (0-394-72674-2).

Gr. 9–12. An anthology of personal accounts by writers, from Doris Lessing to Adrienne Rich, about the "ambivalences and longings" girls feel for their fathers.

Fox, Paula. The Moonlight Man. 1986. Bradbury, $14.95 (0-02-735480-6); Dell, paper, $3.50 (0-440-20079-2).

Gr. 8–12. Catherine spends several weeks alone with her father for the first time since her parents' divorce, and she learns that the man she has always romanticized is intelligent and charming but also desperate.

Frank, Anne. Anne Frank: The Diary of a Young Girl. 1952. Doubleday, $21.95 (0-385-04019-9); Pocket/Washington Square Press, paper, $3.95 (0-685-05466-7).

Gr. 5 and up. In a now classic journal, Anne Frank records intense feelings and observations about her own blossoming adolescence and about the family and friends she lives with as she hides from the Nazis in an Amsterdam attic.

Gaines, Ernest. The Autobiography of Miss Jane Pittman. 1971. Doubleday, o.p.; Bantam, paper, $4.50 (0-553-26357-9).

Gr. 7–12. Writing in the first person, Gaines tells the story of a courageous black woman who began life as a slave and lived to take part in the civil rights movement of the 1960s.

Garden, Nancy. Annie on My Mind. 1982. Farrar, paper, $3.05 (0-374-40414-3).

Gr. 8–12. Two months into college, Liza Winthrop recalls the bittersweetness of the year past, when she met and fell in love with vibrant Annie Kenyon.

Gingher, Marianne. Bobby Rex's Greatest Hit. 1986. Atheneum, o.p.; Ballantine, paper, $3.95 (0-345-34823-0).

Gr. 9–12. In a warm, funny novel about growing up in North Carolina in the 1950s, Pally has a crush on Bobby Rex all through high school and dreams of escape from her little humdrum town.

Greenberg, Joanne. I Never Promised You a Rose Garden. 1964. Holt, o.p.; NAL/Signet, paper, $4.99 (0-451-16031-2).

Gr. 9–12. An autobiographical novel describes a teenage schizophrenic girl's struggle to leave her private fantasy kingdom; a wise psychiatrist helps her face the harsh challenges of the real world.

Guy, Rosa. The Friends. 1973. Holt, $13.95 (0-8050-1742-9); Bantam, paper, $2.95 (0-553-26519-9).

Gr. 6–9. Loneliness draws Phyllisia, a well-to-do West Indian girl, into a mismatched friendship with Edith, a poor classmate from Harlem.

Hall, Lynn. The Solitary. 1986. Macmillan, o.p.; Macmillan/Collier, paper, $2.95 (0-02-043315-8).

Gr. 9–12. After graduation, Jane Cahill returns to the backwoods cabin where she once lived, determined to puzzle out whether it is fright or courage born of past rejections that fuels her need for solitude and her quest for self-reliance.

Hamilton, Virginia. Cousins. 1990. Putnam/Philomel, $14.95 (0-399-22164-6); Scholastic, paper, $2.95 (0-590-45436-6).

Gr. 5–8. Cammy hates her beautiful, sweet, smart cousin Patty Ann, but after a terrible accident at day camp, Cammy finds meanness—and courage—where she never expected to.

Humphreys, Josephine. Rich in Love. 1987. Viking, paper, $10 (0-14-017432-X).

Gr. 9–12. Firmly rooted in her South Carolina home, 17-year-old Lucille remains a strong center for her troubled parents and her beautiful, pregnant older sister, as Lucille herself finds passion and self-acceptance.

Kerr, M. E. Dinky Hocker Shoots Smack. 1972. HarperCollins, lib. ed., $14.89 (0-06-023151-3); paper, $2.95 (0-06-447006-7).

Gr. 6–9. Overweight and unhappy, Dinky longs for some attention from her "do-gooder" mother, who seems to have time for everyone but her daughter.

Kincaid, Jamaica. Annie John. 1985. Farrar, $18.95 (0-374-10521-9); NAL, paper, $6.95 (0-452-26016-7).

Gr. 9–12. Sharply etched episodes evoke a young Caribbean girl's rebellion against her mother and her alternately painful and joy-filled passage into adulthood.

Kingston, Maxine Hong. The Woman Warrior: Memoirs of a Girlhood among Ghosts. 1976. Knopf, $24.95 (0-394-40067-4); paper, $3.95 (0-394-72392-9).

Gr. 9–12. A fiercely honest autobiography of growing up Chinese American in California chronicles Kingston's struggle to balance the "ghosts" of her Chinese tradition with her new American values.

Kusz, Natalie. Road Song. 1990. Farrar, $18.95 (0-374-25121-5); HarperCollins, paper, $10 (0-06-097425-7).

Gr. 9–12. Kusz harks back to her growing up in Alaska, where harsh winters, grinding poverty, and the tragic loss of an eye made her strong and bonded her to her family and the land.

Lasky, Kathryn. Beyond the Divide. 1983. Macmillan, $14.95 (0-02-751670-9); Dell, paper, $3.25 (0-440-91021-8).

Gr. 6–10. Lasky uses a pioneer trek to California as a metaphor for growing up, in a richly textured historical novel about the Amish girl Meribah, who evolves from innocent to self-sufficient woman.

Lord, Bette Bao. Spring Moon: A Novel of China. 1981. HarperCollins, paper, $5.50 (0-06-100105-8).

Gr. 9–12. Spring Moon, though intellectual and educated, suffers the bound feet and other traditional bonds of Chinese women—and then sees her rebellious daughter join the Long March of 1934–35.

McCaffrey, Anne. Dragonsong. 1976. Atheneum, $16.95 (0-689-30507-9); Bantam, paper, $3.50 (0-553-23460-9).

Gr. 6–10. Forbidden to play music because she is a girl, Menolly runs away, becomes telepathically joined to a group of small fire-lizards, and finally is honored for her music at the place of the great dragonriders on the planet Pern.

McCorkle, Jill. Ferris Beach. 1990. Algonquin, $18.95 (0-945575-39-4); Ballantine/Fawcett, paper, $4.99 (0-449-21996-8).

Gr. 9–12. Katie Burns, narrator of this quietly evocative coming-of-age novel set in the South during the 1960s and 1970s, changes from a shy nine-year-old to a sociable teenager who is eventually reconciled with her enigmatic mother.

McCullers, Carson. The Member of the Wedding. 1946. Houghton, o.p.; Bantam, paper, $4.50 (0-553-25051-5).

Gr. 7–12. Frankie Adams, a bored, imaginative 13-year-old, determines not to be left behind when her brother and his bride leave on their honeymoon.

McFadden, Cyra. Rain or Shine. 1986. Knopf, paper, $4.95 (0-394-74879-4).

Gr. 9–12. A frank, fast-talking memoir describes the painful ambivalence a daughter feels for the father she cannot please.

McKinley, Robin. Deerskin. 1993. Berkley/Ace, $17.95 (0-441-14226-5).

Gr. 9–12. After being brutally raped by her father because she has grown up to resemble her dead mother, Princess Lissar flees into the mountains with her loyal dog, Ash, where the pair manage to survive to embark on a series of astounding adventures.

McKinley, Robin. The Hero and the Crown. 1985. Greenwillow, $15.75 (0-688-02593-5); Berkley/Ace, paper, $4.99 (0-441-32809-1).

Gr. 7–12. Aerin, an outsider princess in the mythical land of Damar, fights Maur, the Black Dragon, and becomes the savior of the kingdom.

Mahy, Margaret. The Catalogue of the Universe. 1986. Atheneum/Margaret K. McElderry, $15.95 (0-689-50391-1); Penguin/Puffin, paper, $3.99 (0-14-036600-8).

Gr. 7–12. Rejected when she finally meets the father she's never known, high-school senior Angela finds love with brilliant, homely Tycho, who shares her excitement for science.

Markandaya, Kemala. Nectar in a Sieve. 1955. Day, o.p. NAL, paper, $5.99 (0-451-16836-4).

Gr. 9–12. Married at the age of 12, the peasant girl Rukmani struggles quietly and courageously against personal pressures and against the adversity she encounters in a changing, rural India.

Mason, Bobbie Ann. In Country. 1985. HarperCollins, paper, $10 (0-06-091350-9).

Gr. 9–12. Sam's father died in Vietnam before she was born, and after her high-school graduation, she tries to find out about the war and about her father—wanting to make sense of the world and who she is.

Mazer, Norma Fox. Up in Seth's Room. 1979. Delacorte, paper, $7.95 (0-385-29058-6).

Gr. 9–12. Certain she wants to remain a virgin, Finn has to balance her love for handsome 19-year-old Seth against her need to govern her own body and her own desires.

Mothers and Daughters: That Special Quality: An Exploration in Photographs. 1987. Aperture; dist. by Farrar, paper, $17.50 (0-89381-379-6).

Gr. 9–12. Superb photographs celebrate the mother-daughter bond across a wide range of class, race, and age, with poetry and prose by great writers.

Namioka, Lensey. April and the Dragon. 1994. Harcourt, $10.95 (0-15-276644-8).

Gr. 7–12. Caught between cultures, Chinese American high-school junior April Chen has to relinquish activities important to her to care for her ailing "Dragon Lady" grandmother, even though her brother, Harry, is Grandma's favorite; however, surprisingly, help comes from April's widowed father.

O'Neal, Zibby. The Language of Goldfish. 1989. Viking, $14.95 (0-670-41785-8); Penguin/Puffin, paper, $3.99 (0-14-034540-X).

Gr. 7–10. Carrie finds solace in her artistic abilities, when, unable to handle the changes of growing up, she suffers a nervous breakdown.

Paterson, Katherine. Lyddie. 1991. Dutton/Lodestar, $15 (0-525-67338-5); Penguin/Puffin, $3.99 (0-14-034981-2).

Gr. 7–10. Having lost her parents and seen her brother and sister adopted, 13-year-old Lyddie Worthen, "plain as sod," goes to work in a mill in nineteenth-century Boston but is still able to enrich her mind and exercise her will.

Peck, Richard. Are You in the House Alone? 1976. Viking, $15 (0-670-13241-1); Dell, paper, $3.50 (0-440-90227-4).

Gr. 8–10. Gail Osburne is raped by a boy she knows, but because she is taking the pill and because the accused is one of the richest, most popular boys in her school, she cannot get people to believe her story.

Pei, Lowry. Family Resemblances. 1986. Random, paper, $6.95 (0-394-75528-6).

Gr. 9–12. In a small Illinois town, Karen learns from her unconventional aunt and from her own intimate experience about the sad secrets of adult passion and uncertainty.

Plath, Sylvia. The Bell Jar. 1963. HarperCollins, o.p.; Bantam, paper, $5.99 (0-553-27835-5).

Gr. 9–12. An autobiographical novel about a young girl—brilliant, beautiful, and successful but slowly breaking down—written by a poet who later committed suicide.

Plummer, Louise. My Name Is Sus5an Smith: The 5 Is Silent. 1991. Delacorte, $15 (0-385-30043-3); Dell, paper, $3.50 (0-440-21451-3).

Gr. 9–12. After winning the master's award at the all-high-school art show with an ancestral family portrait that disturbs some family members and after graduating from high school, Sus5an Smith goes to stay in Boston with her aunt, hoping not only for a more exciting life, bit also to find her idealized, long-gone uncle, Willy.

Portis, Charles. True Grit. 1968. Simon & Schuster, o.p.; NAL/Signet, paper, $3.95 (0-451-16022-3).

Gr. 8–12. In an Old West yarn that mixes the comic with the typical shoot-'em-up, a stubborn 14-year-old manipulates an equally stubborn marshal into helping her track down her father's killer.

Rendell, Ruth. The Crocodile Bird. 1993. Crown, $20 (0-517-59576-1).

Gr. 10–12. Past and present meld as resilient, nearly 17-year-old Liza learns to live in the world, for which she's unprepared, and recounts to her lover the tale of her isolated childhood and her mother's obsession and acts of murder.

Roiphe, Anne. Lovingkindness. 1987. Summit, o.p.; Warner, paper, $4.95 (0-446-35274-8).

Gr. 9–12. A radical feminist mother is heartbroken when her daughter joins an Orthodox Jewish sect in Jerusalem and prepares to go through with an arranged marriage.

Sinclair, April. Coffee Will Make You Black. 1994. Hyperion; dist. by Little, Brown, $19.95 (1-56282-796-0).

Gr. 9–12. Jean ("Stevie") Stevenson, a somewhat naive but spunky African American, faces tumultuous friendships, boy problems, uneasy family relationships, and awakening sexuality as she moves from junior high into high school in Chicago between 1965 and 1970.

Smith, Betty. A Tree Grows in Brooklyn. 1943. HarperCollins, paper, $6.50 (0-06-080126-3).

Gr. 7–12. Francie Nolan grows up amid the poverty of a Brooklyn tenement, in a poignant novel set in the early twentieth century.

Staples, Suzanne Fisher. Shabanu. 1989. Knopf, $18 (0-394-84815-2); Random/Vintage, paper, $3.99 (0-679-81030-7).

Gr. 7–12. When after a tragedy, Shabanu, a girl of about 12 living in the present day with her family in the Pakistan desert, is betrothed to a prominent, older man with three wives, she must make a crucial decision: sacrifice herself or dishonor her family. The sequel is *Haveli* (1993).

Tan, Amy. The Joy Luck Club. 1989. Putnam, $18.95 (0-399-13420-4); Random/Vintage, paper, $10 (0-679-72768-X).

Gr. 9–12. These moving, interconnected stories of Chinese American daughters, their mothers, and their grandmothers—in the U.S. and China—speak frankly of the uneasy mix of love, pain, ambition, and family and cultural conflict.

Tepper, Sheri S. Beauty. 1991. Doubleday, $20 (0-385-41939-2); paper, $12 (0-385-41940-6); Bantam, paper, $5.99 (0-553-29527-6).

Gr. 9–12. In an irresistible retelling of "Sleeping Beauty," Beauty is both spunky and sensitive, half-mortal, half-fairy; changing places with her look-alike, illegitimate half-sister, Beloved, who falls into the fated century-long sleep, Beauty is left wide awake and in all kinds of mystifying trouble.

Thesman, Jean. The Rain Catchers. 1991. Houghton, $13.95 (0-395-55333-4); Avon/Flare, paper, $3.50 (0-380-71711-5).

Gr. 8–12. Fourteen-year-old Grayling and her friend Colleen listen as the older women tell stories over cups of steaming tea while waiting for the "honeysuckle rains" to fall the summer that things change and are resolved, letting Colleen and Gray come of age and take their places at the teatime table.

Vail, Rachel. Ever After. 1994. Orchard/Richard Jackson, $15.95 (0-531-06838-2).

Gr. 5–9. In a funny, desperate story about growing up female now, 14-year-old Molly would like to do the right thing, but somehow she always messes up; in the end, her best friend betrays her, and Molly stops being a "nice" girl and cuts loose, starting high school on her own.

Wersba, Barbara. Fat. 1987. HarperCollins, o.p.

Gr. 812. Fat since childhood, 16-year-old Rita has a crush on a trendy young man, until she discovers she loves and is loved by Arnold—gentle, scholarly, eccentric, sexy, and twice her age.

Willey, Margaret. The Bigger Book of Lydia. 1983. HarperCollins, paper, $3.25 (0-06-447049-0).

Gr. 7–12. The friendship that develops between two girls—Lydia, self-conscious about her small size, and anorexic Michelle—helps each girl change her outlook on life.

Wolff, Virginia Euwer. Make Lemonade. 1993. Holt, $15.95 (0-8050-2228-7).

Gr. 7–12. Two inner-city young women ensnared by poverty—17-year-old Jolly, a single-parent mom, and her 14-year-old baby-sitter, LaVaughn—help each other in a riveting story, as disturbing as it is funny and uplifting.

Women & Work: Photographs and Personal Writings. Ed. by Maureen R. Michelson. 1983. NewSage, paper, $22.95 (0-939165-01-5).

Gr. 9–12. Women from 21 to 86 talk about what they do and how they feel about it in a celebration of "women's work" that combines interviews with black-and-white portraits of women in their varied work roles.

Wrede, Patricia C. Dealing with Dragons. 1990. Harcourt/Jane Yolen, $15.95 (0-15-222900-0); Scholastic/Point, paper, $3.25 (0-590-45722-5).

Gr. 6–12. Bored with lessons in dancing, embroidery, drawing, and etiquette and unwilling to marry a dull-witted prince, Princess Cimorene does the unthinkable—she volunteers to be a dragon's captive princess.

Growing Up Male:
Fathers and Sons

When they did the list "Growing Up Female," lack of space prevented compilers Hazel Rochman and Stephanie Zvirin from including all the titles they wanted. So "Growing Up Male" has been broken up into several lists. The first is about boys and their fathers. The son's relationship with his father—the search, the bond, the struggle, the discovery, the leaving—has been part of the coming-of-age myth from Theseus and Telemachus to Baldwin, Hemingway, and Bly. It's also an enduring theme in the contemporary YA novel.

Adler, C. S. Willie, the Frog Prince. 1994. Clarion, $13.95 (0-395-65615-X).

Gr. 4–7. Willie is having a hard time, both in the fifth grade and at home with his dad where Willie can't do anything right, and his too-strict dad gives him very little credit for what he does accomplish.

Baldwin, James. Go Tell It on the Mountain. 1953. Knopf, o.p.; Dell, paper, $5.99 (0-440-33007-6).

Gr. 9–12. John's fight with his father is about the black man's view of himself, but it's also about a teenager's struggle against the parent's self-righteous, brutal authority. Baldwin's autobiographical essay "Note of a Native Son" incorporates some of the same themes.

Berry, James. A Thief in the Village and Other Stories. 1988. Orchard, $12.95 (0-531-05745-3); Penguin/Puffin, paper, $4.99 (0-14-034357-1).

Gr. 7–10. "Was I a ugly baby? An' my father didn' like me?" teenager Fanso asks the grandmother who's raised him, in one of these stories set in contemporary Jamaica.

Carter, Alden R. Wart, Son of Toad. 1985. Putnam, o.p.; Berkley, paper, $2.50 (0-425-08885-5).

Gr. 8–12. Steve's dad wants him to go to college, but Steve has very different ideas. His problem is how to turn stubborn Dad around to his way of thinking.

Close, Jessie. The Warping of Al. 1990. HarperCollins/Charlotte Zolotow, $15.95 (0-06-021280-2).

Gr. 8–12. Growing up in a household dominated by an autocratic father, Al derives comfort from his grandmother, Goopie, whose homespun parables help him survive in his dysfunctional family.

Conroy, Pat. The Great Santini. 1976. Old New York Book Shop, $25 (0-937036-00-5); Bantam, paper, $5.99 (0-553-26892-9).

Gr. 9–12. Marine pilot Meecham treats his family as though they were recruits, and his son Ben rebels.

Cormier, Robert. I Am the Cheese. 1977. Pantheon, $18.95 (0-394-83462-3); Dell/Laurel Leaf, paper, $3.50 (0-440-94060-5).

Gr. 7–12. As Adam rides his bike in search of his missing father, he confronts his own terrifying predicament. Cormier's *After the First Death* is a taut thriller of terrorism and betrayal, told alternately by teenage Ben and his father.

Crutcher, Chris. Running Loose. 1983. Greenwillow, lib. ed., $13.95 (0-688-02002-X); Dell/Laurel Leaf, paper, $3.50 (0-440-97570-0).

Gr. 7–12. With his father's support, 17-year-old Louis Banks defies his racist football coach and copes with the grief that follows his girlfriend's accidental death.

Haynes, David. Right by My Side. 1993. New Rivers; dist. by Talman, paper, $9.95 (0-89823-147-7).

Gr. 9–12. African American teenager Marshall Field Finney describes the year his mother ran away to Las Vegas to find herself, leaving him and his father, Big Sam, to cope on their own.

Howker, Janni. Isaac Campion. 1986. Greenwillow, $10.25 (0-688-06658-5); Dell/Yearling, paper, $2.95 (0-440-40280-8).

Gr. 6–10. In a northern England industrial town around 1900, a boy is driven from home by his father's harshness. Howker's *Nature of the Beast* is about a boy's relationship with his father and grandfather, who become enraged and embittered after being laid off.

Kerr, M. E. The Son of Someone Famous. 1974. HarperCollins, paper, $3.95 (0-06-447069-5).

Gr. 7–10. Adam is the son of a TV celebrity, and he doesn't want anyone in town to know it.

Klein, Norma. No More Saturday Nights. 1988. Knopf, $12.95 (0-394-81944-6); Ballantine/Fawcett Juniper, paper, $3.95 (0-449-70304-5).

Gr. 9–12. Single-parent Tim, 17, takes his baby with him to college in his freshman year.

Koertge, Ron. The Boy in the Moon. 1990. Little, Brown/Joy Street, $14.95 (0-316-50102-6); Avon/Flare, paper, $3.25 (0-590-42412-2).

Gr. 9–12. High-school senior Nick likes and respects his police chief father, even though Nick wishes his dad wouldn't embarrass him about his lack of sexual experience. In Koertge's *Harmony Arms*, teenage Gabriel goes to L.A. with his father (and his dad's hand puppet, Timmy) rather than spend the summer with his mother and her new boyfriend.

Lipsyte, Robert. One Fat Summer. 1977. HarperCollins, lib. ed. $14.89 (0-06-023896-8); paper, $3.95 (0-06-447073-3).

Gr. 7–10. His father's expectations are a heavy burden for overweight Bobby Marks until he learns that being thin and tough isn't nearly as important as doing the right, compassionate thing.

Miller, Arthur. Death of a Salesman. 1949. American Reprint, $16.95 (0-89190-729-7); Penguin, paper, $6 (0-14-048134-0).

Gr. 9–12. An aging salesman faces the truth about himself and tries to make peace with his grown sons, whose lives have been colored by his skewed expectations.

Myers, Walter Dean. Somewhere in the Darkness. 1992. Scholastic, $14.95 (0-590-42411-4); paper, $3.25 (0-590-42412-2).

Gr. 7–12. In this story of a boy, his escaped-con father, and their journey together from New York City to Chicago, then down to the father's childhood home in Arkansas, teenage Jimmy Little sees the failure of his father's dreams, both in prison and out.

Naylor, Phyllis. The Keeper. 1986. Atheneum, $14.95 (0-689-31204-0).

Gr. 6–10. Nick's father is going crazy, but he won't seek help. There's a wall around his father that Nick "couldn't get around or through or over."

Newton, Suzanne. I Will Call It Georgie's Blues. 1986. Viking, o.p.; Penguin/Puffin, paper, $3.95 (0-14-034536-1).

Gr. 8–10. The town minister bullies his family, and although Neal, 15, has a secret escape through music from the rage and pain in his home, his fragile little brother is breaking down.

Paterson, Katherine. The Sign of the Chrysanthemum. Illus. by Peter Landa. 1973. HarperCollins/Crowell, lib. ed., $14.89 (0-690-04913-7); paper, $3.95 (0-06-440232-0).

Gr. 5–7. Growing up in bitter poverty in twelfth-century Japan, Muna believes his father is a great samurai warrior and runs away to find him.

Peck, Richard. Father Figure. 1978. Viking, $15 (0-670-30930-3); Dell/Laurel Leaf, paper, $3.50 (0-440-20069-5).

Gr. 7–12. Jim Atwater's plans to continue as substitute father for his eight-year-old brother must be shoved aside when the boys' real dad comes back into their lives.

Peck, Robert Newton. A Day No Pigs Would Die. 1972. Knopf, $20 (0-394-48235-2); Dell/Laurel Leaf, paper, $3.50 (0-440-92083-3).

Gr. 7–12. In Shaker New England, 12-year-old Robert gets his first taste of adult responsibility when his father tells him he must kill his pet pig.

Potok, Chaim. The Chosen. 1967. Knopf, $29.50 (0-679-40222-5); Ballantine/Fawcett, paper, $5.95 (0-449-21344-7).

Gr. 9–12. Reuven has a good relationship with his father, who encourages him to speak freely. His friend Danny's father is a respected Hasidic rabbi, but he's raised Danny in stern, cold silence.

Renault, Mary. The King Must Die. 1958. Pantheon, $15.95 (0-394-43195-2); paper, $7.95 (0-394-75104-3).

Gr. 9–12. In a thrilling retelling of the Theseus myth, the young man, small and quick-witted, goes on a perilous journey to Athens to find his father—and his own destiny.

Roth, Henry. Call It Sleep. 1960. Pageant, o.p.; Farrar, $30 (0-374-11819-1); paper, $13 (0-374-52292-8); Avon/Bard, paper, $4.95 (0-380-01002-X).

Gr. 9–12. An immigrant Jewish boy grows up in the slums of New York City, nurtured by his gentle, loving mother, terrorized by his father.

Salassi, Otto. On the Ropes. 1981. Greenwillow, paper, $4.95 (0-688-11500-4).

Gr. 6–9. To save the family farm, 11-year-old Squint must find his estranged father, who, as the manager of a motley group of professional wrestlers, turns out to have lots of ideas for keeping creditors at bay.

Santiago, Danny. Famous All over Town. 1983. Simon & Schuster, o.p.; NAL/Plume, paper, $9 (0-452-25974-6).

Gr. 8–12. In a tender, funny novel, Mexican American Chato, 14, is pressured by his father and by the neighborhood gang to be macho and violent.

Shannon, George. Unlived Affections. 1989. HarperCollins/Charlotte Zolotow, lib. ed., $12.89 (0-06-025305-3).

Gr. 8–12. When Willie finds a packet of his father's letters to Willie's mother, he learns about love, about leaving and the fear of being left, and also about lies.

Simon, Neil. Brighton Beach Memoirs. 1984. Random, $14.95 (0-394-53739-4); NAL/Signet, paper, $4.99 (0-451-14765-0).

Gr. 9–12. In this critically acclaimed play, 15-year-old Eugene, preoccupied largely with sex and baseball, still has time to write about his father and the other members of his extended family.

Spiegelman, Art. Maus: A Survivor's Tale. 1986. illus. Pantheon, paper, $12 (0-394-74723-2).

A grim, complex graphic novel in which the cartoonist confronts his difficult

Growing Up Is Hard to Do

relationship with his father and his father's desperate story of Holocaust survival.

Stone, Bruce. Half Nelson, Full Nelson. 1985. HarperCollins, paper, $2.95 (0-06-447047-4).

Gr. 7–10. When his 270-pound father's dream of big-time wrestling causes his mother to leave home, taking his seven-year-old sister along, Nelson Gato sets out to reunite his family.

Theroux, Paul. The Mosquito Coast. 1982. Houghton, o.p.; Avon, paper, $5.95 (0-380-61945-8).

Gr. 9–12. Fourteen-year-old Charlie Fox records how things go awry when his disgruntled father takes his family off into the jungles of Honduras to rediscover a simpler life and unspoiled values.

Todd, Leonard. Squaring Off. 1990. Viking, $13.95 (0-670-83377-0).

Gr. 8–12. In a wild and gentle farce about love and boxing in Georgia in the 1950s, Willie, 13, wants to fight his macho, ex-marine widower father for the affections of Miss Lujane Jessup, the local stripper.

Townsend, John Rowe. Downstream. 1987. HarperCollins/Lippincott, o.p.

Gr. 9–12. English teenager Alan is enraged when he discovers that the woman he loves is having an affair with his father.

Van Raven, Pieter. A Time of Troubles. 1990. Scribner, $13.95 (0-684-19212-8).

Gr. 6–10. Traveling across the desolate Dust Bowl during the 1930s Depression, hoping to find work in California, Roy, 14, must grow up fast and father his irresponsible dad.

Voigt, Cynthia. The Runner. 1985. Atheneum, $14.95 (0-689-31069-2); Ballantine/Fawcett Juniper, paper, $3.95 (0-449-70294-4).

Gr. 7–12. In his fierce battles with his bullying father, loner Bullet Tillerman is determined to break away and run his own life, just as he runs cross-country and eventually chooses to enlist and fight in Vietnam. Also in the Tillerman series is Sons from Afar.

Growing Up Male: Friends

A friend, like a good story, can make the world bigger. Stories of friendship—between young and old, girl and boy, alike or different—are of universal interest to young people, whether the focus is on the conflict between family and friend, the search for identity and courage, the joy of sharing, or the sadness of growing apart. Walter Dean Myers says that when kids write to him about his books what they talk about most is the friendship between characters. Compilers Hazel Rochman and Stephanie Zvirin have searched out some of the most appealing friendship stories.

Avi. "Who Was That Masked Man, Anyway?" 1992. Orchard/Richard Jackson, $14.95 (0-531-08607-0); Avon/Camelot, paper, $3.99 (0-380-72113-9).

Gr. 5–7. With his trusty sidekick, Mario, sixth-grader Frankie Wattleson tries to transform his life into a script from "Captain Midnight" and "Superman." Told through dialogue, this story captures the way kids play.

Bauer, Marion Dane. On My Honor. 1986. Clarion, $13.95 (0-89919-439-7); Dell, paper, $3.25 (0-440-46633-4).

Gr. 5–7. Twelve-year-old Jess has every intention of riding straight to the park as he promised his father, until his assertive friend Tony convinces him otherwise—with tragic results.

Brooks, Bruce. The Moves Make the Man. 1984. HarperCollins, $15 (0-06-020709-4); paper, $3.95 (0-06-447022-9).

Gr. 7–12. Jerome, the first black to integrate a white school, knows the moves you need to survive—in basketball and with people—but his fragile white friend, Bix, refuses to learn how to fake.

Cadnum, Michael. Breaking the Fall. 1992. Viking, $15 (0-670-84687-2).

Gr. 8–12. According to Stanley's troubled friend, Jared, breaking into houses is a game, and Stanley learns to love the wild exhilaration even though he knows it's a game he's bound to lose.

Cole, Brock. The Goats. 1978. Farrar, $15 (0-374-32678-9); paper, $3.95 (0-374-42575-2).

Gr. 6–9. Two outsiders, Howie and Laura, become friends and take care of each other after a vicious practical joke at their summer camp drives them to run away.

Conley, Jane Leslie. Crazy Lady! 1993. HarperCollins/Laura Geringer, $13 (0-06-021357-4).

Gr. 5–8. A big, clunky boy, who's failing seventh grade, befriends the neighborhood drunk "crazy lady," helps her care for her severely disabled son, and watches her ill-fated struggle to keep a home together.

Crutcher, Chris. Staying Fat for Sarah Byrnes. 1993. Greenwillow, $14 (0-688-11552-7).

Gr. 7–12. Overweight Eric ("Moby") Calhoun is the only friend of Sarah Byrnes, who has lived her life behind a mask of burn scars and fury, and when she's hospitalized, seemingly in a catatonic state, Eric visits her every day.

Crutcher, Chris. Stotan! 1986.
Greenwillow, $12 (0-688-05715-2);
Dell, paper, $3.50 (0-440-20080-6).

Gr. 8–12. In a forceful story that combines the energy of sports action with the tragedy of death, four boys on a high-school swim team gradually become friends and support each other when it's discovered that one of them has cancer.

Fox, Paula. Monkey Island. 1991.
Orchard/Richard Jackson, $14.95
(0-531-05962-6); Dell, paper, $3.99
(0-440-407702).

Gr. 5–12. When 11-year-old Clay is abandoned by his parents and finds himself living on the streets of New York City, two street people, teenage Buddy and retired schoolteacher Calvin, share their place in the park with Clay and watch over him the best they can.

Gordon, Sheila. Waiting for the Rain.
1987. Orchard, $12.95
(0-531-05726-7); Bantam, paper, $3.99
(0-553-27911-4).

Gr. 7–12. An interracial friendship is wrenched apart by politics in this compelling story of two teenagers who find themselves fighting on opposite sides in apartheid South Africa.

Hamilton, Virginia. The Planet of Junior Brown. 1971. Macmillan, $14.95
(0-02-742510-X); paper, $3.95
(0-02-043540-1).

Gr. 7–12. In a stirring story of friendship in a scary world, two outsiders—Buddy Clark, who has no family, and Junior Brown, a 300-pound musical prodigy on the run from his overprotective mother—find a home together with other outcasts in an abandoned building.

Hurwitz, Johanna. The Up & Down Spring. 1993. illus. Morrow, $14
(0-688-11922-0).

Gr. 3–6. Roddy and Derek look forward to a great reunion when their friend Bolivia invites them to visit her during spring break. As luck would have it, nothing goes

as planned. Like previous books in the series, this is full of good laughs.

Kimble, Bo. For You, Hank: The Story of Hank Gathers and Bo Kimble. 1992.
Delacorte, $18 (0-385-30389-Q); Dell, paper, $4.99 (0-440-21459-9).

Gr. 8 and up. In a poignant, unpretentious memoir, Kimble pays tribute to Hank Gathers, his childhood friend and teammate, who died on the basketball court during their senior year in college.

Knowles, John. A Separate Peace. 1960.
Macmillan, o.p.; Bantam, paper, $3.95
(0-553-28041-4).

Gr. 7 and up. Gene Forrester harks back to a tragic year during World War II, vividly recalling Phineas, his best friend and roommate at a New Hampshire boarding school touched by the specter of war.

Koertge, Ron. The Boy in the Moon.
1990. Little, Brown/Joy Street, $15.95
(0-316-50102-6); Avon/Flare, paper,
$3.99 (0-380-71474-4).

Gr. 9–12. When Nick's longtime buddy returns home changed after spending the summer with his dad, and Nick's brilliant friend Frieda suddenly begins to make him feel passionate and sexy, he starts to realize that some things are more important than his acne and his physique.

Kordon, Klaus. Brothers Like Friends. Tr.
by Elizabeth D. Crawford. 1992.
Putnam/Philomel, $14.95
(0-399-22137-9).

Gr. 6–10. East Berlin in 1950 is the setting for this story of 17-year-old Frank and his older half-brother, Burkie, the very best of friends. When Burkie is critically hurt in a soccer accident, he swears Frank to secrecy, until it's too late—Burkie dies, and Frank blames himself.

Mahy, Margaret. Underrunners. 1992.
Viking, $14 (0-670-84179-X).

Gr. 5–9. In a thrilling story of friendship and terror in New Zealand, Mahy makes daily life as weird and scary as science fiction. Two friends are kidnapped at gunpoint by a menacing stalker, elegant, crazy, and violent. In Mahy's *Memory* (1987), the poignant friendship is between a drifting teenager and a woman with Alzheimer's disease.

Mowry, Jess. Way Past Cool. 1992. Farrar, $17 (0-374-28669-8); HarperCollins, paper, $10 (0-06-097545-8).

Gr. 9 and up. Friendship takes on new meaning in this tough, riveting story set in a California ghetto, a place where 12-year-old boys deal for Uzis and gang culture recognizes a moral difference between killing and murder.

Myers, Walter Dean. Scorpions. 1988. HarperCollins, $13 (0-06-024364-3); paper, $3.95 (0-06-447066-0).

Gr. 5–10. A strong friendship across cultures is at the center of a moving story about 12-year-old Jamal and his best friend, Tito, who are struggling to survive on dangerous inner-city streets. Many of Myers' stories are about friendship, including the stark novel *Fallen Angels* (1988), about a Harlem teenager fighting in Vietnam, and the funny neighborhood comedy *Fast Sam, Cool Clyde, and Stuff* (1974).

Namioka, Lensey. Yang the Youngest and His Terrible Ear. 1992. illus. Little, Brown/Joy Street, $13.95 (0-316-59701-5); Dell/Yearling, paper, $3.50 (0-440-40917-9).

Gr. 4–7. In this warm, funny immigrant story, two friends who can't live up to the pressures of their rigid families help each other find self-acceptance.

Paterson, Katherine. Bridge to Terabithia. 1977. HarperCollins/Crowell, $14 (0-690-01359-9); paper, $3.95 (0-06-440184-7).

Gr. 5–8. Jess is furious when the new girl, Leslie, beats him in a crucial race; but the two become close friends and make a secret place deep in the woods where no one can come and mess up their games.

Paulsen, Gary. Harris and Me: A Summer Remembered. 1993. Harcourt, $13.95 (0-15-292877-4).

Gr. 6 and up. Dumped on yet another distant relative's doorstep—this time the Larsons' farm—the 11-year-old narrator spends an incredible summer filled with both backbreaking work and the antics of the irrepressible, nine-year-old Harris.

Peck, Richard. Remembering the Good Times. 1985. Delacorte, $14.95 (0-385-29396-8); Dell, paper, $3.50 (0-440-97339-2).

Gr. 6–10. Buck remembers his friendship with Trav and how they both loved the same girl, their classmate Kate.

Peck, Robert Newton. Soup. 1974. Knopf, $9.99 (0-394-92700-1); Dell, paper, $3.25 (0-440-48186-4).

Gr. 4–7. In the first book in a popular middle-grade series, Peck strings together lively reminiscences about the good times he had with his boyhood friend Soup.

Philbrick, Rodman. Freak the Mighty. 1993. Scholastic/Blue Sky, $13.95 (0-590-47412-X).

Gr. 7–10. Big for an eighth-grader, Max feels enormous as well as dumb and tainted by the reputation of his father, Killer Kane; but when Kevin, born with a growth-stunting birth defect, moves nearby, the two boys become friends; and with Kevin providing the brains and imagination and Max the locomotion, they become "Freak the Mighty."

Potok, Chaim. The Chosen. 1967. Knopf, $29.50 (0-679-40222-5); Ballantine/Fawcett, paper, $5.95 (0-449-21344-7).

Gr. 8 and up. Baseball is the bridge to friendship in a story of two teenage players from rival Jewish schools in New York City during World War II. The boys begin as enemies and end up as close friends who sustain each other through hard times.

Growing Up Is Hard to Do

Remarque, Erich Maria. All Quiet on the Western Front. Tr. by A. W. Wheen. 1929. Little, Brown, $18.95 (0-316-73992-8); Ballantine/Fawcett, paper, $4.95 (0-449-21394-3).

Gr. 8 and up. This classic about German teenage soldiers during World War I is about high-school kids who find themselves fighting in a war they know nothing about against an enemy just like them.

Schami, Rafik. A Hand Full of Stars. Tr. by Rika Lesser. 1990. Dutton, $14.95 (0-525-44535-8); Penguin/Puffin, paper, $4.50 (0-14-036073-5).

Gr. 7–10. This warm story of friendship in a multicultural community in contemporary Damascus is set against a background of political terror.

Slepian, Jan. The Alfred Summer. 1980. Macmillan, $12.95 (0-02-782920-0).

Gr. 5–8. Lester is clever, funny, and sensitive, but most people don't know it because his cerebral palsy makes it difficult for him to talk. He feels dependent and frustrated but finds freedom helping three other outsiders in a daring project.

Soto, Gary. Baseball in April and Other Stories. 1990. Harcourt, $14.95 (0-15-205720-X); paper, $4.95 (0-15-205721-8).

Gr. 5–9. Many of these short stories about growing up Latino in Fresno, California, are funny and touching friendship stories, great for reading aloud.

Swarthout, Glendon. Bless the Beasts and Children. 1970. Doubleday, o.p.; Simon & Schuster, paper, $4.50 (0-671-72644-7).

Gr. 8 and up. A group of unhappy teenage boys, the outsiders at a summer camp, find self-respect, freedom, and friendship working together to free a herd of buffalo about to be slaughtered.

A Time to Talk: Poems of Friendship. Ed. by Myra Cohn Livingston. 1992. Macmillan/Margaret K. McElderry, $12.95 (0-689-50558-2).

Gr. 7–12. Classical and new, these poems from many times and places express how friends bring us joy and support; how they betray us and leave us; how we miss them when they're gone. Livingston's *I like You, If You Like Me* (1987) is a friendship anthology for younger readers.

Twain, Mark. The Adventures of Huckleberry Finn. 1885. Many editions are available.

Gr. 7 and up. In Twain's classic friendship story, a trip down the Mississippi River gives runaway Huck a chance to get to know, like, and respect his companion, Jim, an escaped slave.

Voigt, Cynthia. David and Jonathan. 1992. Scholastic, $14.95 (0-590-45165-0).

Gr. 8–12. A Gentile from an old Yankee family, living on Cape Cod in the 1950s, Henry, 16, has been close to his Jewish friend Jon since fifth grade. When Jon's cousin David, a disturbed Holocaust survivor, moves in, all their lives are darkened forever, and Henry finds himself in a struggle with demonic David for Jon's soul.

Who Do You Think You Are? Stories of Friends and Enemies. Ed. by Hazel Rochman and Darlene McCampbell. 1993. Little Brown/Joy Street, $15.95 (0-316-75355-6).

Gr. 7–12. Fifteen stories and autobiographical excerpts by leading American writers, including Maya Angelou, John Updike, Sandra Cisneros, Louise Erdrich, and Richard Peck, explore friendship in the lives of young people and show that sometimes we are friends and enemies, both at once.

Zindel, Paul. The Pigman. 1968. HarperCollins, $14 (0-06-026827-1); Bantam, paper, $3.99 (0-553-26321-8).

Gr. 7–12. John and Lorraine befriend old Mr. Pignati, whom they nickname Pigman, and thoughtlessly betray him with an act that hastens his death.

Growing Up Male: Boys in Love

From Heathcliff on the desolate moors to Bingo Brown in a middle-school classroom, boys in books find themselves swept away: obsessed and infatuated; passionate, romantic, and muddled.

There aren't nearly as many books about boys in love as there are about girls (there are even *fewer* good books about boys and sex), but whether that is the cause or effect of boys reading less is hard to know. Even with more books today about boys' feelings, the male bonding is usually with buddies and the breaking away is from family; if there's a love interest, it's a minor part of the story, while the major focus is on getting to know Dad or on finding oneself through solitary struggle. If there's a girl in this sort of story, she is usually waiting on the sidelines as therapist or supporter.

But compilers Hazel Rochman and Stephanie Zvirin did find some good books about boys in love. Here are some of the best, classic and contemporary, for many age groups and many moods.

Baldwin, James. If Beale Street Could Talk. 1974. Dial, o.p.; Dell, paper, $5.99 (0-440-34060-8).

Gr. 9–12. Fonny, wrongly imprisoned for rape, and Tish, who's pregnant with Fonny's child, support each other in their struggle against injustice and racial oppression in Harlem.

Blume, Judy. Then Again, Maybe I Won't. 1971. Bradbury, $13.95 (0-02-711090-7); Dell, paper, $3.50 (0-440-48659-9).

Gr. 6–9. Along with everything else confusing him when his family moves to an affluent suburb, 13-year-old Tony worries about lust and wet dreams and being a Peeping Tom. He carries a raincoat in case he has a hard-on in class.

Bridgers, Sue Ellen. Permanent Connections. 1987. HarperCollins, $14 (0-06-020711-6); paper, $3.95 (0-06-447020-2).

Gr. 7–12. In trouble with drugs and at school, 17-year-old Rob is sent to live with his father's family in a small Appalachian town. He thinks that a love affair will solve all his problems.

Brontë, Emily. Wuthering Heights. 1847. Many editions are available.

Gr. 8 and up. Angry outsider Heathcliff loves Cathy passionately; together they run wild on the moors in defiance of convention and authority.

Byars, Betsy C. The Burning Questions of Bingo Brown. 1988. Viking, o.p.; Penguin/Puffin, paper, $3.99 (0-14-032479-8).

Gr. 4–6. Middle-schooler Bingo has never been in love before, but one day in English class, he falls in love with three different girls. He's sure that this is love for eternity. Maybe even infinity. Is he ready for mixed-sex conversation?

Clements, Bruce. Tom Loves Anna Loves Tom. 1990. Farrar, $13.95 (0-374-37673-5); paper, $3.95 (0-374-46939-9).

Gr. 7–10. "Nobody in the world is like Anna. I don't mean she's the best person that ever lived, but she's the best person I ever knew." Because Tom loves Anna he tries to protect her in every way he can.

Cooper, Ilene. Choosing Sides. 1990. illus. Morrow, $12.95 (0-688-07934-2); Penguin/Puffin, paper, $3.99 (0-14-036097-2).

Gr. 4–6. Jonathan's life is complicated by sports and by girls—especially by Robin, who is more interesting than basketball.

Dreiser, Theodore. An American Tragedy. 1925. Bentley, $32 (0-8376-0424-9); NAL, paper, $4.95 (0-451-52204-4).

Gr. 10 and up. Clyde loves and is loved by Roberta, his co-worker in the factory, but he's dazzled by a rich girl from the country-club set, and pregnant Roberta stands in his way.

Endo, Shusaku. When I Whistle. Tr. by Van C. Gessel. 1979. Taplinger, paper, $6.95 (0-8008-8244-X).

Gr. 9–12. As he watches his son sell himself for success, a father remembers how he and a close friend loved the same girl in pre–World War II Japan.

Erdrich, Louise. The Bingo Palace. 1994. HarperCollins, $23 (0-06-017080-8).

Gr. 10–12. Readers of Erdrich's previous books, especially *Love Medicine* (1984), will have no trouble relating to the comic yet heartbreaking struggle of Lipsha Morrisey to win the love of teen mother Shawnee Ray Toose.

Finney, Jack. Time and Again. 1970. illus. Simon & Schuster, paper, $10.95 (0-671-24295-4).

Gr. 9–12. As part of a top-secret government project, Simon Morley steps back in time to New York City of the 1880s, where he meets and falls in love with Julia.

Greene, Constance C. The Love Letters of J. Timothy Owen. 1986. HarperCollins, paper, $2.75 (0-06-447026-1).

Gr. 7–10. Instead of approaching the girl of his dreams, a lovesick teenager sends her notes he's cribbed from a book of famous love letters. What a mistake.

Hemingway, Ernest. A Farewell to Arms. 1929. Scribner, $14.95 (0-684-10236-6); Macmillan/Collier, paper, $5.95 (0-02-051900-1).

Gr. 10–12. In the confusion and horror at the World War I Italian front, a wounded American ambulance driver falls passionately in love with a Scottish nurse.

Holland, Isabelle. The Man without a Face. 1972. HarperCollins/Lippincott, $12.95 (0-397-32264-X); paper, $3.95 (0-06-447028-8).

Gr. 7–10. Lonely and troubled about school and home, Charles, 14, reaches out to his tutor, Justin McLeod, and they have one loving night together before they part.

Jones, Diana Wynne. Castle in the Air. 1991. Greenwillow, $13.95 (0-688-09686-7).

Gr. 7–12. Acquiring a threadbare flying carpet, a young merchant sets out to rescue the girl of his dreams from a mighty djinn.

Jordan, June. His Own Where. 1971. HarperCollins/Crowell, $11.95 (0-690-38133-6).

Gr. 8–12. In a lyrical love story written in poetic black English, 16-year-old Buddy tries to make a life for himself and his girl, Angela, in the wilderness of the inner city.

Kerr, M. E. Fell. 1987. HarperCollins/ Charlotte Zolotow, lib. ed., $12.89 (0-06-023268-4); paper, $3.95 (0-06-447031-8).

Gr. 7–12. In a story of love and mystery, Fell is tempted and betrayed by a rich girl with secrets.

Kidd, Ronald. Sammy Carducci's Guide to Women. 1991. Dutton/Lodestar, $14.95 (0-525-67363-6).

Gr. 4–6. After taking pointers from his brother on how to treat women, sixth-grader Sammy Carducci picks the prettiest girl in the class to be his girlfriend.

Klein, Norma. Give and Take. 1985. Viking, o.p.; Ballantine/Fawcett Juniper, paper, $3.99 (0-449-70153-0).

Gr. 9–12. During the summer before college, Spence learns about sex and caring as he is pursued by ex-classmate Taffy and develops a close physical relationship with experienced Audrey.

Koertge, Ron. The Arizona Kid. 1988. Little, Brown/Joy Street, $14.95 (0-316-50101-8); Avon/Flare, paper, $3.50 (0-380-70776-4).

Gr. 7–12. While spending the summer with his gay uncle, Billy falls in love with Cara Mae and gets to know his caring relative and comes to respect his wisdom about "all kinds of love."

Lawrence, D. H. Sons and Lovers. 1913. Many editions are available.

Gr. 10–12. Paul Morel is so tied to his mother that he finds it hard to have a full, loving relationship with the young woman he's close to.

Le Guin, Ursula K. The Beginning Place. 1980. HarperCollins, paper, $6.95 (0-06-091665-6).

Gr. 7–12. In a story that is as much romance as fantasy, Hugh and Irena are brought together by their reponsibility to save the magic world beyond the "beginning place."

Lehrman, Robert. Juggling. 1982. Harper, o.p.

Gr. 8–12. Howard Berger has two goals: he wants to attend a university where he can receive special sports training, and he wants to overcome his shyness with girls and get on with his sexual education.

Lowry, Lois. Your Move, J. P. 1990. Houghton, $13.95 (0-395-53639-1); Dell, paper, $3.50 (0-440-40497-5).

Gr. 5–7. Seventh-grader J. P. is desperately in love with his new classmate, Angela. He'll even use his mother's deodorant to make certain he's presentable.

Mahy, Margaret. The Catalogue of the Universe. 1986. Macmillan/Margaret K. McElderry, $15.95 (0-689-50391-1); Penguin/Puffin, paper, $3.99 (0-14-036600-8).

Gr. 7–12. Tycho has always shared with Angela his excitement about science and ideas, but he thinks of himself as short and ugly, and when she tells him she admires his brilliant mind, he replies (only half-jokingly): "I'd rather be tall."

Mathabane, Mark and **Mathabane, Gail.** Love in Black and White. 1992. illus. HarperCollins, paper, $11 (0-06-092371-7).

Gr. 9–12. In a true story, Mark (who wrote *Kaffir Boy*, a story about his growing up under apartheid) and Gail, a white American minister's daughter, talk candidly about their interracial love and marriage in the U.S.

Maugham, W. Somerset. Of Human Bondage. 1915. Many editions are available.

Gr. 10–12. A disabled young artist fights to overcome the torments of his youth while his obsessive love for a manipulative woman nearly destroys him.

Mazer, Harry. I Love You, Stupid! 1981. HarperCollins/Crowell, o.p.; Avon/Flare, paper, $3.50 (0-380-61432-4).

Gr. 9–12. High-school senior Marcus Rosenbloom knows there are more important things in life than sex, but his imagination still runs wild when he sees or thinks about girls. Then he discovers he loves the girl next door.

Myers, Walter Dean. Motown & Didi: A Love Story. 1984. Viking, $14.95 (0-670-49062-8); Dell, paper, $3.50 (0-440-95762-1).

Gr. 8–12. Two Harlem teens fall in love as they each try to fight the drug culture and poverty around them.

Peck, Robert Newton. Soup in Love. 1992. Delacorte, $14 (0-385-30563-X).

Gr. 4–6. Soup and Rob learn that kissing is "doggone near almost as good" as baseball in a wacky yarn in which the boys decide to impress their girlfriends by winning first prize in a Valentine's Day contest.

Powell, Randy. Is Kissing a Girl Who Smokes Like Licking an Ashtray? 1993. Farrar, $15 (0-374-33632-6); paper, $3.95 (0-374-43627-4).

Gr. 7–12. High-school senior Biff, who's never had a girlfriend, meets beautiful, wild Heidi, whose cigarettes stink up his car and who's also a loner; but these two smart outsiders, awkwardly groping through inhibition and meanness, still come together for a funny romance full of yearning and candor.

Pringle, Terry. The Preacher's Boy. 1988. Algonquin, $15.95 (0-912697-77-6); Ballantine, paper, $4.95 (0-345-36045-1).

Gr. 10–12. To his preacher-father's dismay, sex becomes part of Michael's life when he has a passionate love affair with Amy, a would-be rock 'n' roller.

Raymond, Patrick. Daniel and Esther. 1990. Macmillan/Margaret K. McElderry, $13.95 (0-689-50504-3).

Gr. 7–12. When Daniel falls in love with Esther at their progressive boarding school in England, the pair must face the agony of her return to Hitler's Austria.

Roth, Philip. Goodbye, Columbus. 1959. Houghton, o.p.; Bantam, paper, $4.50 (0-553-26365-X).

Gr. 9–12. A poor, young, Jewish librarian has a sexually intense affair with a beautiful girl whose newly rich family has recently moved to the suburbs.

Sachs, Marilyn. The Fat Girl. 1984. Dutton, $13.95 (0-525-44076-3); Dell, paper, $2.75 (0-440-92468-5).

Gr. 7–12. Jeff's obsession with an unhappy fat girl moves from revulsion to fascination as he tries to take control of her life and make her beautiful.

Strasser, Todd. A Very Touchy Subject. 1986. Delacorte, o.p.; Dell, paper, $2.95 (0-440-98851-9).

Gr. 8–12. Scott decides that the sexually experienced girl who lives next door is just the right person to help him figure out the difference between sex and love.

Townsend, Sue. The Secret Diary of Adrian Mole, Aged 13 3/4. 1986. Grove, o.p.; Avon/Flare, paper, $4.99 (0-380-86876-8).

Gr. 7–12. "There is a new girl in our class. She sits next to me in Geography. She is all right. . . . I might fall in love with her." Adrian Mole would like to be an intellectual, but he has all kinds of problems, with his acne, his girlfriend, and his parents.

Ure, Jean. You Win Some, You Lose Some. 1986. Delacorte, $14.95 (0-385-29434-4); Dell, paper, $2.95 (0-440-99845-X).

Gr. 7–10. Jamie Carr has come to London to win a place in a prestigious ballet school and to find a girlfriend, but his romantic dreams about the girls in his class don't quite work out.

Vail, Rachel. Do-Over. 1992. Orchard/Richard Jackson, $14.95 (0-531-05460-8).

Gr. 5–7. Giving a beguiling, first-person view of a boy's first crush, first kiss, first heartbreak, and first real boy-girl relationship, this poignant, comical novel captures the pain and pleasure of being 13.

Wrede, Patricia C. Searching for Dragons. 1991. Harcourt/Jane Yolen, $16.95 (0-15-200898-5); Scholastic/Point, paper, $3.25 (0-590-45721-7).

Gr. 7–12. Mandanbar, king of the Enchanted Forest, and Cimorene, a dragon's pretty chief cook and librarian, borrow a flying carpet and set off in search of the king of the dragons—along the way, they fall in love.

Growing Up Male: Boys in Love

Growing Up an Outsider

The outsider theme—both heroic and painful—has elemental appeal for YAs as they struggle with their complex needs for individual identity and community. This updated bibliography is based on "The Outsider: Hero, Stranger, Freak," compiled by Hazel Rochman for the June 1, 1988, issue of *Booklist*. The aim continues to be to suggest the diversity—from adventure in space, wilderness, and war, to personal struggle with friends, lovers, family, and within the self; hence, the inclusion of a wide range of books on the outsider theme—mainly fiction, YA and adult, classic and contemporary—for a wide variety of tastes and reading.

Achebe, Chinua. Things Fall Apart. 1959. Astor-Honor, $12.95 (0-8392-1113-9); paper, $7.95 (0-8392-5008-8). Other editions are available.

Gr. 9–12. With the coming of the Europeans to Nigeria at the turn of the century, the old ways break down, and traditional Okonkwo is alienated from his son, who converts to Christianity.

Avi. Wolf Rider. 1986. Bradbury, $14.95 (0-02-707760-8); paper, $3.95 (0-02-041513-3).

Gr. 6–9. When teenager Andy gets a telephone call warning of a murder, no one believes him, not the police, not the victim (who isn't dead—not yet), not his own father.

Baldwin, James. Go Tell It on the Mountain. 1953. Knopf, o.p.; Dell, paper, $5.99 (0-440-33007-6).

Gr. 9–12. John's fight with his father is about the black man's view of himself; it is also about John's struggle against his parents' self-righteous and brutal authority.

Bell, Clare. Ratha's Creature. 1983. HarperCollins/Margaret K. McElderry, o.p.; Dell, paper, $2.95 (0-440-97298-1).

Gr. 7–10. Millions of years ago in a society of intelligent wild cats, Ratha is driven from the pack when she discovers how to tame fire and challenges the leader.

Brooks, Bruce. The Moves Make the Man. 1984. HarperCollins, $15 (0-06-020709-4); paper, $3.95 (0-06-447022-9).

Gr. 6–10. Jerome, the first black to integrate a white school, knows the moves you need to survive, but his fragile white friend, Bix, refuses to learn how to fake.

Cole, Brock. The Goats. 1987. Farrar, $15 (0-374-32678-9); paper, $3.95 (0-374-42575-2).

Gr. 5–9. A boy and a girl, known as "the goats" at their summer camp, are the victims of a cruel practical joke, but they escape, and as they try to find shelter, they take care of each other.

Conrad, Pam. Prairie Songs. 1985. HarperCollins, paper, $3.95 (0-06-440206-1).

Gr. 5–10. Young Louisa loves the solitude of the wide Nebraskan prairie, but Emmeline, the doctor's wife, can't adjust to the harsh pioneer life, especially to the loneliness.

Conroy, Frank. Body & Soul. 1993. Houghton, $22.95 (0-395-51946-2).

Gr. 10–12. A fatherless street urchin,

Claude Rawlings is blessed with remarkable talent and a nurturing mentor, both of which enable the lonely boy to find himself and fame through music.

Cormier, Robert. I Am the Cheese. 1977. Pantheon, $18.95 (0-394-83462-3); Dell, paper, $3.99 (0-440-94060-5).

Gr. 7–12. In a dark thriller, a boy being questioned by a government agency struggles to discover who he is and how he got there.

Crew, Linda. Children of the River. 1989. Delacorte, $14.95 (0-440-50122-9); Dell, paper, $3.50 (0-440-21022-4).

Gr. 6–10. Cambodian refugee Sundara wants to fit in with the crowd in her Oregon high school, but she's caught between feeling too American at home and not American enough at school.

Cross, Gillian. Chartbreaker. 1987. Holiday, $14.95 (0-8234-0647-4); Dell, paper, $2.95 (0-440-20312-0).

Gr. 7–10. Teenage rock star Finch, vulnerable and ugly, sings like concentrated danger, her performance charged with rage and with her love for the bandleader.

Dickens, Charles. Great Expectations. 1861. Many editions available.

Gr. 8–12. An escaped convict—"a fearful man all in coarse gray, with a great iron on his leg"—grabs young Pip in the graveyard and continues to haunt him as he struggles to become a gentleman and win the heart of beautiful, rich Estella.

Du Maurier, Daphne. Rebecca. 1938. Doubleday, $25 (0-385-04380-5); Avon, paper, $4.95 (0-380-00917-X).

Gr. 8–12. Poor, plain, and alone, a young woman marries a rich widower, but in his great English country house, she feels she can't live up to his dazzling first wife, Rebecca—and then a terrible secret is revealed.

Eckert, Allan. Incident at Hawk's Hill. 1971. Little, Brown, $15.95 (0-316-20866-3); Bantam, paper, $3.99 (0-553-26696-9).

Gr. 6 and up. Awkward with people but close to animals, Ben is a stange, shy little boy, and when he is lost on the Canadian prairie, a badger cares for him for two months.

Fox, Paula. One-eyed Cat. 1984. Bradbury, $14.95 (0-02-735540-3); Dell, paper, $3.99 (0-440-46641-5).

Gr. 5–9. Ned has a guilty secret that he feels separates him from his parents who believe he is loving and good.

Golding, William. Lord of the Flies. 1954. Coward, o.p.; Putnam, paper, $4.95 (0-399-50148-7).

Gr. 8–12. Marooned on a tropical island, a group of English schoolboys try to set up an ordered society, but most of them descend into savagery and begin to hunt each other to the death.

Guest, Judith. Ordinary People. 1976. Viking o.p.; Penguin, paper, $6.95 (0-14-099718-0).

Gr. 9–12. Teenage Conrad, home from the hospital after attempting suicide, is painfully trying to pick up his life again, feeling like a stranger at home and at school.

Guy, Rosa. The Disappearance. 1979. Delacorte, $9.95 (0-385-28129-3); Dell, paper, $3.50 (0-440-92064-7).

Gr. 7–10. After being taken in by a middle-class family, inner-city teenager Imamu must find their missing child—to save himself from being the accused.

Hall, Lynn. Just One Friend. 1985. Scribner, o.p.; Macmillan/Collier, paper, $2.95 (0-02-043311-5).

Gr. 7–10. Though sensitive and strong, Dory is mentally slow. "One of the worst things about being dumb in a regular school is that the other kids get the idea that you don't have any feelings."

Hamilton, Virginia. Anthony Burns: The Defeat and Triumph of a Fugitive Slave. 1988. Knopf, $12.95 (0-394-88185-0); paper, $3.99 (0-679-83997-6).

Gr. 7–10. As he waits in jail and then is tried in the Boston Court House, and as his case galvanizes the abolitionist movement, young escaped slave Anthony Burns remembers his life in bondage and his struggle to be free.

Holman, Felice. Slake's Limbo. 1974. Scribner, $13.95 (0-684-13926-X); Macmillan/Adladdin, paper, $3.95 (0-689-71066-6).

Gr. 5–9. Scorned and tormented at school and on the streets, orphaned Slake feels he is a worthless lump until one day when the gangs are after him, he takes refuge in the subway, where he makes a home for himself.

Jenkins, Lyll Becerra de. The Honorable Prison. 1988. Dutton/Lodestar, $14.95 (0-525-67238-9); Penguin/Puffin, paper, $3.95 (0-14-032952-8).

Gr. 7–12. In a terrorist Latin American dictatorship, Marta's father is a threat to the state, and the family is placed under house arrest in a remote region.

Jones, Diana Wynne. Howl's Moving Castle. 1986. Greenwillow, lib. ed., $13 (0-688-06233-4).

Gr. 7–12. Sophie, the eldest of three daughters, knows that according to fairy-tale convention, she's expected to fail first and worst, so she doesn't even try; but when a witch's curse turns her into a feisty old woman, she finds the energy to hobble out into the unknown.

Kerr, M. E. Fell. 1987. HarperCollins/Charlotte Zolotow, lib. ed., $12.89 (0-06-023268-4); paper, $3.95 (0-06-447031-8).

Gr. 6–12. Fell, a policeman's son, is out of his class when he gets involved with a girl in the rich crowd of his resort town.

Kerr, M. E. Night Kites. 1986. HarperCollins/Charlotte Zolotow, lib. ed., $14.89 (0-06-023254-4); paper, $3.95 (0-06-447035-0).

Gr. 8–12. "I never like anything too exotic or oddball," says preppy Erick, before he discovers that his beloved brother, Pete, is gay and suffering from AIDS.

Kingston, Maxine Hong. The Woman Warrior: Memoirs of a Girlhood among Ghosts. 1976. Knopf, $24.95 (0-394-40067-4); paper, $4.95 (0-394-72392-9).

Gr. 9–12. Kingston describes her conflict growing up Chinese American, caught between the "ghosts" of her Chinese tradition and the alien values of the U.S.

Lee, Gus. China Boy. 1991. Dutton, $19.95 (0-525-24994-X); NAL, paper, $5.99 (0-451-17434-8).

Gr. 9–12. Funny, crude, sad, and ugly, Lee's autobiographical novel tells about growing up "foreign, different, stupid"— until the skinny loser finally learns to speak street language and to fight bullies, racists, and his abusive stepmother.

Lynch, Chris. Iceman. 1994. HarperCollins, $15 (0-06-023340-0).

Gr. 8–12. Knowing that his parents are incapable of giving him the warmth and honest emotion he needs, 14-year-old Eric slams out his anger and suffering in the hockey rink, where he's the Iceman, so out of control even his own teammates shun him.

Lipsyte, Robert. One Fat Summer. 1977. HarperCollins/Charlotte Zolotow, $14.89 (0-06-023896-8); paper, $3.95 (0-06-447073-3).

Gr. 7–10. Overweight Bobby Marks dreads hot weather when he can't hide his fat body, but one summer he slims down as he sticks to an exhausting job, stands up to his father and the local bullies, and finds his own definition of a strong hero.

Mahy, Margaret. Memory. 1988. Macmillan/Margaret K. McElderry, $14.95 (0-689-50446-2); Dell, paper, $3.50 (0-440-20433-X).

Gr. 8–12. Alone in the city night, teenage Jonny, tormented by the memory of his sister's death, meets Sophie, whose memory has been desytroyed by Alzheimer's disease, and they help each other find tenderness in a cruel world.

Mathabane, Mark. Kaffir Boy. 1986. Macmillan, o.p.; NAL/Plume, paper, $9.95 (0-452-25943-6).

Gr. 9–12. This autobiography of a black youth's coming of age in apartheid South Africa depicts a fierce struggle for survival under conditions of overwhelming brutality.

Maugham, W. Somerset. Of Human Bondage. 1915. Many editions available.

Gr. 9–12. Medical student Philip Carey, born with a club foot, struggles for independence and becomes obsessed with a shallow young woman.

McKinley, Robin. Beauty: A Retelling of the Story of Beauty and the Beast. 1978. HarperCollins, $16 (0-06-024149-7); paper, $4.95 (0-06-440477-3).

Gr. 7–12. Forced to come alone to the Beast's great castle, brave Beauty frees him from his hideous enchantment through the power of her love.

Morrison, Toni. Beloved. 1987. Knopf, $27.50 (0-394-53597-9); NAL/Plume, paper, $10 (0-452-26446-4).

Gr. 10–12. The ghost of the child Beloved comes back to haunt the mother who murdered her, in a demanding novel that dramatizes the agony, violence, and sexual abuse of slavery.

Newton, Suzanne. I Will Call It Georgie's Blues. 1983. Viking, o.p.; Penguin/Puffin, paper, $3.95 (0-14-034536-1).

Gr. 8–10. The town minister bullies his family, and though 15-year-old Neal's jazz provides him with a secret escape, his fragile little brother is breaking down.

Oneal, Zibby. In Summer Light. 1985. Viking, $12.95 (0-670-80784-2); Bantam, paper, $3.50 (0-553-25940-7).

Gr. 7–12. Home from school with mono, Kate drifts, lonely, irritable, unable to use her artistic talent, crippled by rage at her famous, domineering artist father.

Orwell, George. 1984. 1949. Many editions are available.

Gr. 8–12. Winston hates the system, hates Big Brother. He knows that his rebellion puts him in terrible danger and that the Thought Police will find him.

Paterson, Katherine. Jacob Have I Loved. 1980. HarperCollins/Crowell, $14 (0-690-04078-4); paper, $3.95 (0-06-440368-8).

Gr. 7–12. Plain Louise feels deprived of schooling, friends, mother, and even her name by her pretty twin sister.

Paulsen, Gary. Hatchet. 1987. Bradbury, $14.95 (0-02-770130-1); Penguin/Puffin, paper, $3.99 (0-14-032724-X).

Gr. 6–10. Surviving a plane crash, Brian finds himself alone in the Canadian wilderness.

Pomerance, Bernard. The Elephant Man. 1979. Grove, paper, $7.25 (0-394-17539-5).

Gr. 9–12. A play based on the life of John Merrick, born with a gross deformity and rescued from a nineteenth-century freak show by a London doctor.

Remarque, Erich Maria. All Quiet on the Western Front. 1929. Several editions are available.

Gr. 9–12. Fighting in the nightmare trenches of World War I, a group of high-school classmates realizes that false patriots sent them to fight for a cause they know nothing about: "We were all at once terribly alone"

Renault, Mary. The King Must Die. 1958. Pantheon, $15.95 (0-394-43195-2); paper, $7.95 (0-394-75104-3).

Gr. 9–12. Small, quick-witted young Theseus must undertake a perilous journey to Athens to find his father and his own heroic identity.

Rendell, Ruth. The Crocodile Bird. 1993. Crown, $20 (0-517-59576-1).

Gr. 10–12. Resilient, nearly 17-year-old Liza learns to live in the world and recounts to her lover the tale of her isolated childhood and her mother's obsession and acts of murder.

Santiago, Danny. Famous All over Town. 1983. Simon & Schuster, o.p.; NAL/Plume, paper, $9.95 (0-452-25974-6).

Gr. 8–12. Fourteen-year-old Chato, gifted and sensitive, is pressured by the machismo of his father and the neighborhood gang, in a humorous, moving novel about a Mexican American family in Los Angeles.

Sebestyen, Ouida. Words by Heart. 1979. Atlantic Monthly, o.p.; Bantam, paper, $3.99 (0-553-27179-2).

Gr. 7–10. In 1910, young Lena Sills and her family are the first blacks to move into a small western town, where some of the whites feel threatened by the Sills and use violence to drive them out.

Shelley, Mary. Illus. by **Moser, Barry.** Frankenstein. 1984. Univ. of California/Pennyroyal, $35 (0-520-05281-1).

Gr. 9–12. A modern, large-size edition, in which Moser's woodcuts express the horror of the monster as well as the suffering of the outsider driven away by those he would love.

Sillitoe, Alan. The Loneliness of the Long-distance Runner. 1960. Knopf, $18.95 (0-394-43389-0); NAL/Signet, paper, $3.50 (0-451-16831-6).

Gr. 9–12. In a long short story, a teenager in an English reformatory turns out to be a champion runner with a chance to win the trophy for his team, but as he trains, he plans a perfect way to defy the powerful who have always excluded him.

Sleator, William. House of Stairs. 1974. Dutton, $14.95 (0-525-32335-X); Penguin/Puffin, paper, $3.95 (0-14-034580-9).

Gr. 7–12. Five teenage orphans find themselves in an indoor place with no walls, ceiling, or floor—only stairs—where they are the subjects of a diabolical experiment.

Spinelli, Jerry. There's a Girl in My Hammerlock. 1991. Simon & Schuster, $13 (0-671-74684-7); paper, $3.95 (0-671-86695-8).

Gr. 5–9. Gender can make you an outsider. Maisie Brown goes out for junior-high wrestling—to the consternation of her brother, the boys on the team, and most of the school.

Swarthout, Glendon. Bless the Beasts and Children. 1970. Doubleday, o.p.; Simon & Schuster, paper, $4.50 (0-671-72644-7).

Gr. 8 and up. The misfits in a tough, competitive summer camp out West find self-respect working together to free a herd of buffalo about to be slaughtered.

Tempest, John. Vision of the Hunter. 1989. HarperCollins, o.p.; Pocket, paper, $4.95 (0-671-69409-X).

Gr. 7–12. In an exciting and sensitive story of early human society, a young outsider driven from the hunting tribe at a time of great scarcity, saves his people by leading the way in domesticating the herds.

Twain, Mark. The Adventures of Huckleberry Finn. 1885. Many editions are available.

Gr. 7 and up. With fugitive slave Jim, outcast Huck Finn rafts down the Mississippi, away from those who would "sivilize" him.

Vinge, Joan D. Psion. 1982. Delacorte, $12.95 (0-385-28780-1); Dell, paper, $2.95 (0-440-97192-6).

Gr. 8–12. A slum orphan of dual human-alien heritage, 16-year-old Cat becomes involved in a psi research project that leads to a telepathic confrontation with a deadly psion intent on dominating the universe.

Voigt, Cynthia. The Runner. 1985. Atheneum, $14.95 (0-689-31069-2); Ballantine/Fawcett Juniper, paper, $3.95 (0-449-70294-4).

Gr. 7–12. Bullet runs 10 miles a day and is state champion, but only in cross-country, never track; fierce and apart, he is determined that no one will box him in.

Wolff, Virginia Euwer. Probably Still Nick Swansen. 1988. Holt, $13.95 (0-8050-0701-6); Scholastic, paper, $2.95 (0-590-43146-3).

Gr. 7–12. Caught between his limitations and his longing to experience life like everyone else, special-education student Nick Swansen invites a former classmate to the prom and is devastated when she stands him up.

Woodson, Jacqueline. Maizon at Blue Hill. 1992. Delacorte, $14 (0-385-30796-9); Dell, paper, $3.50 (0-440-40899-7). .

Gr. 5–10. Seventh-grader Maizon Singh, black and smart, leaves her Brooklyn neighborhood to take up a scholarship in a private Connecticut girls' boarding school; but she can't fit in. For the first time in her life she's a "minority," and she hates it.

Wright, Richard. Black Boy. 1945. HarperCollins, paper, $6 (0-06-081250-8).

Gr. 10–12. Wright's autobiography describes his childhood and teenage years in the brutally racist South, where, though he was forced to mask his pride in himself, "It had never occurred to me that I was in any way an inferior being."

Zindel, Paul. David & Della. 1993. HarperCollins, $15 (0-06-023353-2).

Gr. 7–12. Repressed David and outrageous Della meet when David, a high-school playwright, decides he needs a coach to help him overcome his writer's block; as it turns out Della, an alcoholic, needs David as much as he needs her.

Growing Up Gay Aware

Gay people make up a small but significant minority in American society, but because of discrimination, they are often still reluctant to "come out of the closet." Lacking visible role models, many teenagers turn to books, often library books, for their first information about same-sex attractions. The lives of contemporary teens are touched by gay and lesbian issues and people in many ways. Young people may have gay family members, friends, or neighbors. Many more are affected by anti-gay prejudice—from the teens who are harassed for not adhering to their peers' sex-role stereotypes to those who treat "gay-bashing" as acceptable behavior. Books containing gay/lesbian characters or concerns may counter the stereotypes commonly expressed in the media and by peers.

The following selective bibliography, an adapted and updated version of "Being Gay: Gay/Lesbian Characters and Concerns in Young Adult Books," originally compiled by Christine Jenkins, lists gay-inclusive young adult fiction and nonfiction. Unfortunately, the list of available books is inclusive only up to a point: few portray people of color, and more than two-thirds of the gay people represented in these titles are male. In reality, lesbians and gay men belong to all races, ethnic groups, and classes and live in all regions of the country.

Fiction

Am I Blue? Ed. by Marion Dane Bauer. 1994. HarperCollins, $15 (0-06-024253-1).

Gr. 7 and up. Sixteen stories by as many authors—a number of whom will be familiar to young adult readers—explore the gay and lesbian experience. In some a teenager grapples with his or her own sexuality; in others a young person has a loved one—a parent or a friend—who is homosexual.

Block, Francesca Lia. Weetzie Bat. 1989. HarperCollins/Charlotte Zolotow, $12.95 (0-06-020534-2); paper, $3.95 (0-06-447068-7).

Gr. 8 and up. This unusual fairy tale set in the Los Angeles punk/new wave scene features Weetzie and Dirk, two teenagers searching for true love. Weetzie finds the mysterious Secret Agent Lover Man; Dirk finds the attractive surfer Duck; and the two couples—one straight, one gay—create a home for themselves and each other.

Brett, Catherine. S. P. Likes A. D. 1989. The Women's Press; dist. by Inland, paper, o.p.

Gr. 8 and up. Stephanie (S. P. of the title) doesn't know why she is so taken with a female classmate (A. D.), but she worries about the intensity of her feelings. Then Stephanie gets to know two of her mother's friends, whose warm relationship gives her a model for mature love.

Bunn, Scott. Just Hold On. 1982. Delacorte, paper, $9.95 (0-385-28490-X).

Gr. 8 and up. Stephen and Charlotte, drawn together in mutual support as they deal with their troubled parents (Stephen's father is an alcoholic; Charlotte is an incest victim), become part of a tight group of friends who accept Stephen and Rolf when they become lovers.

Chambers, Aidan. Dance on My Grave. 1982. HarperCollins/Charlotte Zolotow, paper, spring 1995, $3.95 (0-06-447135-7).

Gr. 9 and up. Hal, 16, meets handsome, dashing Barry and is amazed by the immediate attraction between them. Their relationship ends prematurely when Barry dies in a motorcycle accident, a stereotypically tragic end that flaws an otherwise fine coming-of-age story told in a sharply humorous narrative voice.

Childress, Alice. Those Other People. 1989. Putnam, $14.95 (0-399-21510-7).

Gr. 8 and up. A contemporary novel told from a variety of viewpoints: from the gay teenager who has left home to find himself, to the black teenager whose family has just moved to an all-white neighborhood, to the young woman who has a reputation for being easy, to the high-school teacher who thinks he's justified in copping a feel. All have their own voices and their own very definite opinions of "those other people."

Donovan, John. I'll Get There, It Better Be Worth the Trip. 1969. HarperCollins, o.p.

Gr. 6 and up. Davy is a troubled and isolated 13-year-old whose delight in a new friendship is seriously disturbed when a friendly wrestling match between the boys turns into a kiss. This is considered a groundbreaking book, the first YA novel to deal directly with same-sex attractions.

Ecker, B. A. Independence Day. 1983. Avon, paper, o.p.

Gr. 7 and up. When Mike begins to think he might be gay, he never dreams he'll have the courage to come out to his best friend, Todd, but when Mike finally does, Todd not only reaffirms their friendship, but also offers to help Mike tell his parents.

Futcher, Jane. Crush. 1981. Alyson, paper, $7.95 (1-55583-139-7).

Gr. 8 and up. A senior at a girls' boarding school in the mid-1960s, Jinx is fascinated by the talented and beautiful Lexie, but rigid school rules and Lexie's taste for crazy escapades prove to be the girls' undoing.

Garden, Nancy. Annie on My Mind. 1982. Farrar, paper, $3.95 (0-374-40414-3).

Gr. 7 and up. When Liza and Annie, two New York City high-school seniors meet, they are immediately drawn to each other. Although both young women face conflicts in accepting their feelings of attraction, the story captures the magic and intensity of first love.

Guy, Rosa. Ruby. 1977. Viking o.p.; Dell, paper, $3.50 (0-440-21130-1).

Gr. 8 and up. Ruby, the youngest daughter in a West Indian family that moves to Harlem, is attracted to self-confident, beautiful, and upwardly mobile Daphne. Their vaguely drawn romance is short-lived, but Daphne's influence on Ruby is ultimately positive, and Ruby faces her own future with growing self-esteem.

Hall, Lynn. Sticks and Stones. 1977. Follett, o.p.

Gr. 7 and up. Tom is welcomed as a newcomer at a rural Iowa high school until his friendship with a boy who is rumored to be gay stigmatizes him in the eyes of the community. The author paints a stark and thought-provoking picture of homophobia in this novel about the motivation and destructive power of gossip.

Hautzig, Deborah. Hey, Dollface. 1978. Greenwillow, lib. ed. $11.88 (0-688-84170-8).

Gr. 7 and up. New students at an exclusive private high school, Val and Chloe feel like outsiders in a world of debutantes and status-conscious classmates. Their outcast status draws them together, and the story of their friendship is a funny, tender narrative about the difficult process of growing up.

Holland, Isabelle. The Man without a Face. 1972. HarperCollins/Lippincott, $12.89 (0-397-32264-X); paper, $3.95 (0-06-447028-8).

Gr. 7 and up. Charles needs a summer tutor and finds one in Justin, a reclusive retired teacher with a mysterious past. His house becomes a haven for Charles, and although Justin's Mr. Rochester–like persona reinforces the gayness-as-tragic-flaw stereotype, readers will probably find him as intriguing as Charles does.

Homes, A. M. Jack. 1989. Macmillan, $14.95 (0-02-744831-2); Random/Vintage, paper, $10 (0-679-73221-7).

Gr. 8 and up. Jack is a witty, tough-talking son of divorced parents whose life is disrupted when his father comes out to him. Jack's anger ("I stayed in my room all night, trying to figure out how my father could be queer. I mean, historically, queers are not fathers") eventually dissipates as Jack adjusts to this new information.

Kerr, M. E. I'll Love You When You're More Like Me. 1977. HarperCollins, paper, $3.50 (0-06-447004-0).

Gr. 7 and up. Three young people face problems as they confront parental and societal expectations: Wally is at odds with his father, Sabra is trying to ease out from under her mother's domination, and Charlie is the town outcast for telling his family he "believed he preferred boys to girls."

Kerr, M. E. Nightkites. 1986. HarperCollins/Charlotte Zolotow, lib. ed., $14.89 (0-06-023254-4); paper, $3.95 (0-06-447035-0).

Gr. 9 and up. Erick is 17 when he learns that his older brother, Pete, is gay and has AIDS. The negative impact on Erick and his parents is considerable and, at times, unrelievedly grim, but Pete is a likable character, and he and Erick have a good relationship in a story in which the villain is not only the disease, but also the mindless fear it inspires in the community.

Klein, Norma. Breaking Up. 1980. Random/Pantheon, o.p.; Avon/Flare, paper, $2.50 (0-380-55830-0).

Gr. 8 and up. Ali Rose lives in New York City with her mother, her brother, and her mother's lover, Peggy. While spending the summer with her father and his new wife, Ali is confronted with the fact that her mother and Peggy are more than "just good friends"; her father's resulting hysteria and a threatened custody battle are both alarming and realistic.

Klein, Norma. My Life as a Body. 1987. Knopf, o.p.

Gr. 9 and up. A shy, intelligent girl, Augie falls in love with Sam, a wheelchair-bound classmate. During the span of the novel, Augie, Sam, and Augie's best friend, Claudia, who's "known since she was five that she was gay," leave home for college and continue toward adulthood.

Klein, Norma. Now That I Know. 1988. Bantam, $13.95 (0-553-05472-4); paper, $2.95 (0-553-28115-1).

Gr. 7 and up. Her parents' shared custody arrangement is fine with Nina until her father tells her that he is gay and his lover is moving in with him. Though she worries about sharing her father's attention and about the social stigma of having a gay parent, Nina, after a period of adjustment, is finally able to sort out her own feelings and reconcile with her father.

Koertge, Ron. The Arizona Kid. 1988. Little, Brown/Joy Street, $14.95 (0-316-50101-8); Avon/Flare, paper, $3.50 (0-380-70776-4).

Gr. 7 and up. Billy, 16, spends the summer in Tucson working at a racetrack and getting to know his uncle Wes, whose complete acceptance of his own gay identity and his warm regard for his nephew come through strongly, as does his life in a gay community facing the AIDS crisis.

L'Engle, Madeleine. A House like a Lotus. 1984. Farrar, $17.95 (0-374-33385-8); Dell, paper, $3.99 (0-440-93685-3).

Gr. 8 and up. Suffering the pangs of adolescent gawkiness, Polly O'Keefe (daughter of Meg and Calvin from *A Wrinkle in Time*) is made to feel confident and special by Max, a beautiful and talented artist friend of Polly's family, who lives nearby with Ursula, her companion of 30 years. When Polly learns that Max and Ursula are lovers, the plot becomes something of a soap opera. Still, Polly's maturation in the course of the novel is well done.

Meyer, Carolyn. Elliott and Win. 1986. Macmillan/Margaret McElderry, paper, $3.95 (0-02-044702-7).

Gr. 6 and up. From the moment Win first walks into Elliott's house, he is certain that their relationship as Amigos (a Big Brother–type organization) is going to be a disaster—Elliott cares nothing for team sports, serves gazpacho for lunch, and doesn't even own a television. Though Elliott fits a number of gay male stereotypes, his sexual orientation is never defined, nor is it necessary to do so, since Win finds that forging friendships is more important than fitting the traditional masculine mold.

Mullins, Hilary. The Cat Came Back. 1993. Naiad, $9.95 (1-56280-040-X).

Gr. 7–12. Prep school senior Stevie tells in diary form how she falls in love with her classmate Andrea, from the initial attraction and excitement to the doubt and denial to the tender, passionate love affair.

Murrow, Liza Ketchum. Twelve Days in August. 1993. Holiday, $14.95 (0-8234-1012-9).

When the team bully tries to pit the rest of the team against soccer star Alex by suggesting he's gay and refusing to play with him, 16-year-old Todd, who is attracted to Alex's twin sister, is not ready to befriend or to turn against Alex; only when Todd discovers that his uncle is gay does he stand up for Alex.

Reading, J. P. Bouquets for Brimbal. 1980. Harper, o.p.

Gr. 8 and up. Macy Beacon and Annie Brimbal have been best friends for years, but when they go off to summer stock theater after high-school graduation, their lives begin to separate. Both become romantically involved—Annie with another actress—and Macy finds she must accept Annie's new relationship if their friendship is to continue.

Rees, David. In the Tent. 1971. Alyson, paper, $6.95 (0-932870-75-9).

Gr. 8 and up. Although Tim has been attracted to his friend Aaron for a long time, his strict religious upbringing makes it difficult for him to face his feelings until they join two other boys for a holiday camping trip that turns into an adventure when they get fogbound. This adversity helps Tim accept the fact that he and Aaron have different preferences that may keep them from being lovers—but not from being friends.

Rees, David. The Milkman's on His Way. 1982. Gay Men's Press; dist. by Inland, paper, $7.95 (0-907040-12-8).

Gr. 8 and up. A coming-out, coming-of-age story told by Ewen, a working-class teenager growing up in an isolated English town. At 15, Ewen becomes aware of his attractions to other boys, but this is only the first in a series of steps he must take on his way to maturity and self-acceptance.

Rees, David. Out of the Winter Gardens. 1984. Olive Press, o.p.

Gr. 8 and up. Sixteen-year-old Mike has not seen his father since he was very young. When his father invites him for a visit, Mike learns almost immediately that his father is gay, and the three-week visit changes Mike's life—not in "turning him gay" as his mother feared but in establishing a warm father-son relationship.

Salat, Cristina. Living in Secret. 1993. Bantam/Skylark, $15 (0-553-08670-7).

Though the courts think she's better off with her dad, 11-year-old Amelia wants to live with her lesbian mom, who plans that she and her partner will kidnap Amelia and move to California with new identities; it's not easy living in secret, and before Amelia's dad tracks her down, she learns some important lessons about tolerance, acceptance, truth, and love.

Scoppettone, Sandra. Happy Endings Are All Alike. 1978. Harper, o.p.; Alyson, paper, $6.95 (1-55583-177-X).

Gr. 7 and up. Jaret and Peggy's romantic relationship is thrown into turmoil when Jaret is violently assaulted and raped. Jaret's matter-of-fact acceptance of her own gay feelings is a refreshing change from the torment many fictional gay teenagers go through, and her problems arise from the rape and public reaction to it, rather than from her identity as a lesbian.

Scoppettone, Sandra. Trying Hard to Hear You. 1974. HarperCollins, o.p.; Alyson, paper, $7.95 (1-55583-196-6).

Gr. 7 and up. Camilla tells the story of her close-knit summer stock theater crowd, and of Jeff and Phil, who were part of that crowd—until they fell in love. Though most of their peers react with confusion and hostility, Camilla progresses from shocked disbelief to acceptance.

Shannon, George. Unlived Affections. 1989. HarperCollins/Charlotte Zolotow, o.p.

Gr. 8 and up. After Willy's grandmother/guardian dies, he finds a cache of old letters from his father to his mother. The device of a story told in letters is skillfully done, and Willy becomes acquainted with the father he never knew, a man who had come to terms with his gay sexual preference at the cost of his marriage.

Singer, Marilyn. The Course of True Love Never Did Run Smooth. 1983. HarperCollins, o.p.

Gr. 7 and up. The high school is staging A Midsummer Night's Dream, and various members of the cast and crew are falling in love. There are several true loves in the novel, and though none of their paths is smooth, each pair, gay and straight alike, is certain that their love is right for them.

Snyder, Ann and **Pelletier, Louis.** The Truth about Alex (original title: Counterplay). 1981. NAL, paper, $2.75 (0-451-14996-3).

Gr. 8 and up. Brad is straight and Alex is gay, but their shared interests and football teamwork create a bond that social pressures cannot break. This is a story about male friendship and the rejection faced by boys who refuse to conform.

Ure, Jean. The Other Side of the Fence. 1988. Delacorte, $14.95 (0-385-29627-4).

Gr. 8 and up. Richard leaves home after a quarrel with his parents and picks up hitchhiker Bonny, a tart-tongued, working-class teen, who is also running away. Each helps the other face and overcome parental and societal disapproval; Richard returns to his male lover, Bonny to her foster parents; and the reader sees that people of different backgrounds—both in sexual orientation and class—can enrich each other's lives.

Walker, Kate. Peter. 1993. Houghton, $13.95 (0-395-64722-3).

Gr. 7–12. Am I gay or aren't I? Fifteen-year-old Peter's confused about his sexual identity; he feels pressured to become sexually active, but he's repelled by the approach of a sexually blatant girl; however, there is a girl he really likes; at the same time, he feels some attraction for his older brother's gay friend, David.

Wersba, Barbara. Crazy Vanilla. 1986. HarperCollins/ Charlotte Zolotow, lib. ed., $11.89 (0-06-026369-5).

Gr. 7 and up. At 14 Tyler feels estranged from his father (who is distant), his mother (who is an alcoholic), and his brother, Cameron (who has been banished from the family for being gay). When Tyler first meets Mitzi Gerrard, he is immediately put off by her brash manner and loud mouth, but their mutual interest in photography draws them together, and Tyler is finally able to talk to someone about his feelings and rebuild a relationship with his brother.

Growing Up Is Hard to Do

Wersba, Barbara. Just Be Gorgeous. 1988. HarperCollins/Charlotte Zolotow, lib. ed., $11.89 (0-06-026360-1); Dell, paper, $3.25 (0-440-20810-6).

Gr. 7 and up. A New York City teenager is convinced of her own unattractiveness, but a gay teenage waif who supports himself by tap dancing on the street becomes her best friend, companion, and morale-booster, telling her to "just be gorgeous." Both are determined to be true to themselves, and both find enough of what they are looking for to keep them going.

Nonfiction

Borhek, Mary V. Coming Out to Parents: A Two-Way Survival Guide for Lesbians and Gay Men and Their Parents. 1983. Pilgrim, paper, $9.95 (0-8298-0665-2).

Gr. 8–12. The author brings a knowledge of Christian doctrine and biblical teaching to this self-explanatory book of thoughtful advice. Borhek also wrote *My Son Eric* (Pilgrim 1979), the story of her gradual acceptance of her son's homosexuality.

Cohen, Susan and **Cohen, Daniel.** When Someone You Know Is Gay. 1989. M. Evans, $13.95 (0-87131-567-X); Dell, paper, $3.99 (0-440-21298-7).

Gr. 8–12. Written for teens who have a gay friend or relative, this self-help book dispels common stereotypes with basic information to promote a better understanding of the gay and lesbian experience.

Hyde, Margaret O. and **Forsyth, Elizabeth H.** Know about Gays and Lesbians. 1994. Millbrook, $15.90 (0-56294-298-0).

Gr. 7–12. Making it clear that knowing about homosexuality is a first and crucial step toward furthering dignity for all, the authors attack stereotypes, survey history, examine cultural responses and current controversies (gays in the U.S. military, for example), and review religious responses to homosexuals.

Fairchild, Betty and **Hayward, Nancy.** Now That You Know: What Every Parent Should Know about Homosexuality. Rev. ed. 1989. Harcourt, paper, $8.95 (0-15-667601-X).

Gr. 9–12. This gentle guide contains information and advice to help parents of gays and lesbians understand their children. Although not written specifically for young people, it can serve to facilitate communication between teens and their parents.

Homosexuality: Opposing Viewpoints. Ed. by William Dudley. 1993. Greenhaven, $17.95 (0-89908-481-8); paper, $9.95 (0-89908-456-7).

Gr. 9–12. Typical of the Oppsong Viewpoints series, this offers carefully juxtaposed articles for and against issues regarding homosexuality.

Landau, Elaine. Different Drummer: Homosexuality in America. 1986. Messner, $11.29 (0-671-54997-9).

Gr. 9–12. Landau's introduction to the lives of lesbians and gay men in the U.S. today is written for a young adult audience. Topics covered include relationships with the family, the mental health establishment and the law, and historical and current causes of homophobia; the account also contains several interviews with gay teenagers.

Two Teenagers in Twenty: Writings by Gay and Lesbian Youth. Ed. by Ann Heron. 1994. Alyson, $17.95 (1-55583-229-6).

Gr. 7–12. Adding new testimonies to the plainspoken words she gathered for *One Teenager in Ten* (1983), Heron reveals what it's like to grow up gay and lesbian today—the anxiety and the isolation, but also the determination, the pride, and the relief at discovering the truth about oneself.

Growing Up Gay Aware

Growing Up Religious

Even though the spiritual experience is very much a part of growing up and is the dominant theme in evangelical Christian titles, religion is pretty much ignored in mainstream publishing for young people. That may be because the subject is so controversial—one person's religion is another's myth or superstition. There's censorship pressure from all sides. On the one hand, separation between church and state makes some schools and libraries wary of books about religion. On the other hand, demands by certain religious groups have kept from the shelves books about "heathen" cultures and books that ask questions about everything from witchcraft to evolution. The opposite is true in much mainstream literature about Native Americans, where religion is the only story, as if American Indians are noble stereotypes, not people with ordinary daily experiences.

As always, compilers Hazel Rochman and Stephanie Zvirin looked for books that were good stories, whatever the faith or conflict involved. They found many about growing up Jewish and Christian, but few about the other religions practiced by millions in this country and around the world.

Anaya, Rudolfo A. Bless Me, Ultima. 1972. Tonatiuh-Quinto Sol International, paper, $12 (0-89229-002-1).

Gr. 8–12. One of the most famous and best-selling of Mexican American novels tells the story of the initiation of a young boy, Antonio, through his relationship with Ultima, a wise *curandera* (mentor).

Ashabranner, Brent. Gavriel and Jamal: Two Boys of Jerusalem. Photos by Paul Conklin. 1984. Dodd, o.p.

Gr. 4–8. A moving photo-essay about a Jewish boy and a Palestinian boy growing up in a city holy to Arabs, Jews, and Christians.

Babbitt, Lucy Cullyford. Where the Truth Lies. 1993. Orchard/Richard Jackson, $14.95 (0-531-05473-X).

Gr. 7–10. Religion and fantasy mingle in a provocative novel about three teens—one an atheist, another a polytheist, and a third from a country believing in one god—who seek to overcome the problems of religious intolerance their peoples face.

Baldwin, James. Go tell It on the Mountain. 1953. Knopf, o.p.; Dell, paper, $5.99 (0-440-33007-6).

Gr. 8–12. In a powerful autobiographical novel, teenage John struggles with inner religious conflict and with his rigid evangelist father in 1930s Harlem. John's fight with his father is also about the black man's view of himself.

Barber, Phyllis. How I Got Cultured: A Nevada Memoir. 1992. Univ. of Georgia, $24.95 (0-8203-1413-7).

Gr. 9–12. Insightful without being sentimental, Barber vividly recalls growing up Mormon on the outskirts of Las Vegas during the Eisenhower era.

Beatty, Patricia. Who Comes with Cannons? 1992. Morrow, $14. (0-688-11028-2).

Gr. 5–7. Twelve-year-old Truth Hopkins and her Quaker family face the danger brought to their doorstep by the outbreak of the Civil War in a story that acknowledges the moral and physical courage of people who refused to take sides.

Black Elk. Black Elk Speaks: Being the Life Story of a Holy Man of the Oglala Sioux. As Told through John G. Niehardt. 1932. Univ. of Nebraska, $19.95 (0-8032-3301-9); paper, $9.95 (0-8032-8359-8).
Gr. 8–12. In a book that has become a religious classic, Black Elk, warrior and medicine man of the Oglala Sioux, waiting out his last days on the Pine Ridge Reservation, blends his personal story with his sacred vision.

Blume, Judy. Are You There, God? It's Me, Margaret. 1970. Bradbury, $13.95 (0-02-710991-7); Dell, paper, $3.99 (0-440-40419-3).
Gr. 5–7. Because her father is Jewish and her mother Christian, Margaret doesn't know whether to join the Jewish Community Center or the Y. She asks God for help with her problems. An ever-popular, tender, funny story of contemporary life.

Chambers, Aidan. N.I.K.: Now I Know. 1988. HarperCollins/Charlotte Zolotow, $13.95 (0-06-021208-X).
Gr. 9–12. "I'm not bothered about religion and I don't believe in God," declares skeptical British teenager Nik, whose quest for belief culminates in his own mock crucifixion.

Dana, Barbara. Young Joan. 1991. HarperCollins/Charlotte Zolotow, $17.95 (0-06-021422-8).
Gr. 6–10. A sweet, simple farm girl from the French countryside hears, assimilates, and acts upon a message from God.

Dancing Tepees: Poems of American Indian Youth. Ed. by Virginia Driving Hawk Sneve. Illus. by Stephen Gammell. 1989. Holiday, $14.95 (0-8234-0724-1); paper, $5.95 (0-8234-0879-5).
Gr. 5–9. This is a handsomely produced picture-book anthology of tribal songs and prayers as well as short poems by contemporary tribal poets.

Dickinson, Peter. Tulku. 1979. Dutton, o.p.; Dell, paper, $3.99 (0-440-21489-0).
Gr. 9–12. A 13-year-old orphan enters Tibet with Mrs. Jones and her young lover, where they meet a monastic who believes the baby Mrs. Jones carries is the new Dalai Lama.

du Boulay, Shirley. Tutu: Voice of the Voiceless. 1988. Eerdmans, $22.50 (0-8028-3649-6).
Gr. 7–12. This moving biography of the archbishop of Cape Town and winner of the Nobel Peace Prize integrates his liberation theology with his personal story of growing up Anglican under apartheid.

Fitzgerald, John D. The Great Brain. 1985. Dial, $12.95 (0-8037-3074-8); Dell, paper, $3.99 (0-440-43071-2).
Gr. 4–6. Fitzgerald remembers what it was like to grow up Mormon in Utah at the turn of the century, a constant adversary of his older brother, the Great Brain.

Hesse, Herman. Siddartha. Tr. by Hilda Rosner. 1951. New Directions, $16.95 (0-8112-0292-5); paper, $4.95 (0-8112-0068-X).
Gr. 7–12. In a beautifully told Buddhist allegory set in India, a young man leaves home to find the meaning of life.

Howe, Norma. God, the Universe, and Hot Fudge Sundaes. 1983. Houghton, o.p.; Avon, paper, $2.50 (0-380-70074-3).
Gr. 7–10. Caught between her born-again Christian mother and her cynical father, Alfie reexamines her religious beliefs when she attends a creationist versus evolutionist trial for a school project.

Kerr, M. E. What I Really Think of You. 1982. HarperCollins, $13 (0-06-023188-7); paper, $3.50 (0-06-447062-8).

Gr. 7–12. Several of Kerr's books deal with the subject of religion. In this one, the daughter of Seaville's Holy Roller preacher and the son of a celebrated televangelist are brought together when the preacher's son decides church business will improve if his girlfriend fakes a healing.

Levitin, Sonia. Escape from Egypt. 1994. Little, Brown, $15.95 (0-316-52273-2).

Gr. 8–12. Reaching deeply and often into the Bible to give her novel texture, Levitin humanizes the story of the Israelites' exodus from Egypt by focusing on teenage Hebrew Jesse, who struggles with his attraction for half-Syrian Jennat and with the tenets of a new religion.

Levoy, Myron. Alan and Naomi. 1977. Harper, paper $3.95 (0-06-440209-6).

Gr. 5–9. In New York City in 1944, Alan tries to help troubled Holocaust refugee Naomi, and he questions how God could have allowed such evil to happen.

Logan, Laurel Oke. Janette Oke: A Heart for the Prairie. 1993. Bethany, $15.99 (1-55661-326-1).

Gr. 9–12. The background and growing-up years of one of America's best-known and -loved Christian fiction writers are highlighted in a biography written by Oke's daughter.

Maguire, Gregory. Missing Sisters. 1994. Macmillan/Margaret K. McElderry, $14.95 (0-689-50590-6).

Gr. 6–9. Alice, an orphan with speech and hearing problems, thinks only a miracle can help her feel less lost after a fire injures her elderly friend, Sister Vincent De Paul. That miracle comes in the form of Miami Shaw, an identical twin sister Alice never knew she had.

Marshall, Catherine. Christy. 1967. McGraw-Hill, o.p.; Avon, paper, $5.50 (0-380-00141-1).

Gr. 7–12. A young woman becomes a teacher in a poor area of Appalachia in 1912 in a story of love and idealism and Christian faith.

Mazer, Anne. Moose Street. 1992. Knopf, $13 (0-679-83233-5).

Gr. 5–7. Although not from an observant family, Lena Rosen is Jewish. That makes her an outcast on Moose Street, but it also enables her to see her 1950s neighborhood with clearer vision than others who live there.

McCarthy, Mary Therese. Memories of a Catholic Girlhood. 1957. Harcourt, paper, $8.95 (0-15-658650-9).

Gr. 9–12. In a series of autobiographical pieces, McCarthy describes her orphaned childhood caught between two sets of grandparents and three religions: Catholic, Jewish, and Protestant.

Miller, Arthur. The Crucible. 1953. Viking, o.p.; Penguin, paper $6.50 (0-14-048138-9).

Gr. 8–12. This play based on the Salem witchcraft trials of 1692 focuses on the attack on a nonconformist member of the Puritan community.

Naylor, Phyllis. A String of Chances. 1982. Atheneum, $13.95 (0-689-30935-X).

Gr. 8–12. Sixteen-year-old Evie has never questioned the beliefs of her minister father until she leaves home to spend the summer with a married, pregnant cousin—and tragedy strikes.

Paterson, Katherine. Rebels of the Heavenly Kingdom. 1983. Dutton/Lodestar, $11.95 (0-525-66911-6); Avon/Flare, paper, $2.95 (0-380-68304-0).

Gr. 7–10. Wang Lee, a 15-year-old peasant boy, is caught up in the Taiping Rebellion in China in the 1850s, when hundreds of thousands of the poorest people, fiercely patriotic and imbued with their own version of Christianity, are fighting to free China from the weak and corrupt Manchu regime. Paterson's contemporary novels also frequently deal with religious experience as part of growing up.

Peck, Robert Newton. A Day No Pigs Would Die. 1972. Knopf, o.p.; Dell, paper, $3.50 (0-440-92083-3).

Gr. 7–10. On a Shaker farm in Vermont in the 1920s, teenage Rob must come to terms with issues of life and loss and taking adult responsibility.

Perez, Louis G. The Dalai Lama. 1993. Rourke, $19.93 (0-86625-480-3).

Gr. 6–12. The personal story of the winner of the 1989 Nobel Peace Prize begins with his being discovered, as a baby, to be the reincarnated leader of his country. For younger readers, Lois Raimondo's photo-essay, The Little Lama of Tibet (1994), captures the daily life of the six-year-old boy who is now being trained to be the next high lama in the Tibetan Buddhist religion.

Potok, Chaim. The Chosen. 1967. Knopf, $30 (0-679-40222-5); Fawcett, paper, $5.95 (0-449-21344-7).

Gr. 6–12. A relationship that starts in the fierce rivalry of a baseball game grows into a strong bond between two Orthodox Jewish boys, Danny and Reuven, as Reuven becomes involved in Danny's conflict with his austere, Hasidic rabbi father. The story continues in The Promise.

Powers, John. The Last Catholic in America. 1973. Saturday Review Press, o.p.; Warner, paper, $4.95 (0-446-31252-5).

Gr. 9–12. Powers draws partly on his own memories for this bittersweet novel about growing up Catholic during the 1950s on Chicago's South Side.

Pringle, Terry. The Preacher's Boy. 1988. Algonquin, $15.95 (0-912697-77-6).

Gr. 9–12. A young man rebels against his Baptist minister father, finding solace in sex and in a relationship with an equally rebellious young woman.

Ruby, Lois. Miriam's Well. 1993. Scholastic, $13.95 (0-590-44937-0).

Gr. 7–12. Jewish Adam Bergen thinks Miriam Pellham, diagnosed with bone cancer, will surely die because the small religious sect to which she is devoted prohibits medical intervention.

Rumbaut, Hendle. Dove Dream. 1994. Houghton, $13.95 (0-395-68393-9).

Gr. 5–9. In a small 1960s Kansas town, Dove Derrysaw goes on a vision quest as her Chickasaw ancestors did. Her search is for both mysticism and common sense.

Rylant, Cynthia. A Fine White Dust. 1986. Bradbury, $13.95 (0-02-777240-3); Dell, paper, $3.50 (0-440-42499-2).

Gr. 5–9. Growing up in a North Carolina town, Pete has always been religious, though his parents are not. When an intense revival preacher comes to town, Pete is born again, finding the Preacher Man compelling and mysterious.

Salinger, J. D. Franny & Zooey. 1961. Little, Brown, o.p.; Bantam, paper, $3.95 (0-553-26973-9).

Gr. 10–12. Dissatisfied with herself, 20-year-old Franny thinks the solution to her unhappiness may lie in religion.

Shalant, Phyllis. Shalom, Geneva Peace. 1992. Dutton, $14 (0-525-44868-3).

Gr. 6–9. Joining her synagogue's youth group, Andi meets worldly, rebellious Geneva Peace, who smokes, bad-mouths her stepmother, and chases after the congregation's rabbinical intern.

Some, Malidoma Patrice. Of Water and the Spirit: Ritual, Magic, and Initiation in the Life of an African Shaman. 1994. Putnam/Tarcher, $22.95 (0-87477-762-3).

Gr. 8–12. Kidnapped as a young child in West Africa, Some was trained ("brainwashed") for 15 years in a strict French Catholic mission school and Jesuit seminary, until he rebelled and made his way back through the jungle to his tribal village. There he underwent the traditional month-long Dagara initiation rite; but he never lost his Western education.

Soto, Gary. Home Course in Religion. 1991. Chronicle, paper, $8.95 (0-87701-857-X).

Gr. 7–12. There's anger and fragility in the casual idiom and rhythms of Soto's clear, intimate poems about growing up Catholic and Mexican in California.

Speare, Elizabeth. The Bronze Bow. 1961. Houghton, paper $7.70 (0-395-13719-5).

Gr. 5–8. Vowing vengeance against the Romans he blames for the death of his parents, Daniel bar Jamin finds unexpected solace in the teachings of Jesus, who preaches in Galilee.

Sussman, Susan. There's No Such Thing as a Chanukah Bush, Sandy Goldstein. 1983. Albert Whitman, $8.95 (0-8075-7862-2).

Gr. 3–5. Resigned to the fact that she'll never have a Christmas tree, Robin, who's Jewish, has her hopes raised when she learns Sandy Goldstein is getting a "Chanukah bush."

Temple, Frances. The Ramsay Scallop. 1994. Orchard/Richard Jackson, $17.95 (0-531-06836-6).

Gr. 7–10. Sent on a pilgrimage by their village priest, 14-year-old Elenor and her betrothed, Lord Thomas, who has just returned from a crusade to the Holy Land, come to know themselves and each other as they journey across thirteenth-century France to a shrine in Spain.

Webb, Sheyann and **Nelson, Rachel West.** Selma, Lord, Selma: Girlhood Memories of the Civil Rights Days. 1980. Univ. of Alabama, $12.95 (0-8173-0031-7).

Gr. 6–12. Like many experiences of the civil rights movement, this account is rooted in the church. Webb and Nelson remember themselves at age eight, march-ing, singing, being set upon by troopers, going to meetings, and talking about those who had been jailed or beaten or killed.

Tolan, Stephanie. Save Halloween! 1993. Morrow, $14 (0-688-12168-3).

Gr. 4–7. Her father and her uncle, both preachers, are opposed to celebrating Halloween, but although Johnna is devoted to her religion, she feels differently and struggles to decide what's really right.

X, Malcolm and **Haley, Alex.** The Autobiography of Malcolm X. 1965. Amereon, $21.95 (0-89190-216-3); Ballantine, paper, $5.95 (0-345-35068-5).

Gr. 8–12. Malcolm Little, who became Muslim Malcolm X, evolved from being a teen dope peddler to a leading voice in the Nation of Islam. Whether in the streets of Harlem or on his pilgrimage to Mecca, he was always transforming himself.

West, Jessamyn. Friendly Persuasion. 1945. Harcourt, $10.95 (0-15-133605-9).

Gr. 9–12. Josh, the eldest Birdwell son, must measure his belief in the Union cause against his strict Quaker upbringing and his love for his family.

White, Mel. Stranger at the Gate: To be Gay and Christian in America. 1994. Simon & Schuster, $23 (0-671-88407-7).

Gr. 9–12. Drawing on his experience of growing up gay, religious, and ashamed in a conservative Christian family, White exposes the homophobia of the religious right who denied that his sexuality was "a part of God's creative plan."

Yolen, Jane. The Gift of Sarah Barker. 1980. Viking, o.p.; Penguin/Puffin, paper, $3.99 (0-14-036027-1).

Gr. 7–10. In this bittersweet love story, two teenagers struggle to reconcile the beliefs of their Shaker community with their affection for one another and their growing desire for independence.

Growing Up Jocks

Focusing on autobiography and biography but including some fiction, this retrospective bibliography of mostly recent titles, compiled by Sally Estes, is intended as a companion to and extension of "Playing the Game: Sports Fiction" [BKL Mr 1 87], which was updated for publication in *Genre Favorites for Young Adults: A Collection of Booklist Columns* (1993). Selections range from adult books for YAs to books for middle-school readers.

Aaron, Henry and **Wheeler, Lonnie.** I Had a Hammer. 1991. HarperCollins, paper, $5.99 (0-06-109956-2).

Gr. 9–12. Aaron's story probably tells as much about America and baseball in general as it does about Aaron, who grew up in Alabama—poor, black, but crazy about baseball. *Hank Aaron: Home Run King* (1992), by Jacob Margolies, follows Aaron's professional achievements for middle readers.

Aaseng, Nathan. True Champions: Great Athletes and Their Off the Field Heroics. 1993. Walker, $14.95 (0-8027-8246-9).

Gr. 6–9. Aaseng features athletes who reflect personal courage, compassion, and heroism—the "true champions"—in an inspiring collection of sports profiles.

At the Crack of the Bat. Ed. by Lillian Morrison. 1992. illus. Hyperion; dist. by Little, Brown, $14.95 (1-56282-176-8).

Gr. 4–6. Baseball, in all its running, whacking, heartbreaking, hero-loving glory, is celebrated in this compilation of odes to the sport.

Barkley, Charles and **Johnson, Roy S.** Outrageous! The Fine Life and Flagrant Good Times of Basketball's Irresistible Force. 1992. Simon & Schuster, $20 (0-671-73799-6); Avon, paper, $4.99 (0-380-72101-5).

Gr. 9–12. Barkley's opinionated musings ("professional athletes should not

be role models") enliven an entertaining autobiography in which the controversial, irrepressible basketball star comes off as a genuinely likable person.

Benoit, Joan and **Baker, Sally.** Running Tide. 1987. Knopf, $16.95 (0-394-55457-4).

Gr. 9–12. In a refreshing autobiographical account, 1984 Olympic gold medal marathoner Benoit reflects on a life spent largely in athletic competition, and recounting the skiing accident in 1973 that steered her toward running, sensitively discusses the effects her athletic career has had on her personal life.

Christopher, Matt. Return of the Home Run Kid. 1992. illus. Little, Brown, $14.95 (0-316-14080-5).

Gr. 4–7. In the sequel to *The Kid Who Only Hit Homers* (1972), Sylvester Coddmeyer III finds that he can't seem to hit or field, and dejected, questions his abilities—until, as in the first book, a mysterious adult encourages him to be more aggressive and confident.

Cohen, Neil. Jackie Joyner-Kersee. 1992. illus. Sports Illustrated for Kids; dist. by Little, Brown, paper, $4.95 (0-316-15047-9).

Gr. 4–7. Cohen presents a woman who knows that talent is not enough and who hones her natural ability through training and intelligent analysis in his portrait of the woman who grew up in a poor section of East St. Louis and went on to win two gold medals at the 1988 Olympics.

Connolly, Pat. Coaching Evelyn: Fast, Faster, Fastest Woman in the World. 1991. illus. HarperCollins, $15.95 (0-06-021282-9).

Gr. 7–10. In her account of training Evelyn Ashford (Olympic medal winner in 1984 and 1988), Coach Connolly affords an inside look at a runner's life before and after the starting gun as well as an inspiring portrait of two women drawn together by mutual respect, affection, and the determination to break world records.

Cooper, Ilene. Choosing Sides. illus. 1990. Morrow, $12.95 (0-688-07934-2); Penguin/Puffin, paper, $3.99 (0-14-036097-2).

Gr. 4–6. In the third installment of the Kids from Kennedy Middle School series, Jonathan Rossi has problems: he wants to quit the basketball team but doesn't want to disappoint his dad, who's convinced Jon will be the team's star player.

Dennis, Jerry. A Place on the Water: An Angler's Reflections on Home. 1993. St. Martin's, $19.95 (0-312-09811-1).

Gr. 8–12. Beginning with his childhood fishing with a cane pole and a can of worms, Dennis evokes halcyon days and nights fishing, canoeing, and exploring Michigan waterways.

Deuker, Carl. Heart of a Champion. 1993. Little, Brown/Joy Street, $14.95 (0-316-18166-8).

Gr. 8–10. Baseball has been the basis for Seth and Jimmy's friendship, from their first meeting on a practice field at age 12 through their time together in summer leagues and on high-school teams. A novel full of sports action and playing tips by the author of On the Devil's Court (1989).

Doherty, Craig, and **Doherty, Katherine M.** Arnold Schwarzenegger: Larger than Life. 1993. Walker, $14.95 (0-8027-8238-8).

The Dohertys follow Schwarzenegger's life from his childhood in Austria, discussing his focus and determination as he worked to become a champion in physical fitness and power. Pair this with Lipsyte's Arnold Schwarzenegger: Hercules in America, also published in 1993.

Dygard, Thomas J. Game Plan. 1993. Morrow, $14 (0-688-12007-5).

Gr. 6–9. Student manager of the high-school football team, Beano Hatto is thrust into the spotlight—and onto the hot seat—when the team's coach is injured and Beano gets the job of coaching the team for the big last game, only a week away.

Extra Innings: Baseball Poems. Ed. by Lee Bennett Hopkins. 1993. illus. Harcourt, $14.95 (0-15-226833-2).

Gr. 4–6. A collection of 19 poems about baseball by the likes of May Swenson, Lillian Morrison, Ernest Thayer, and the editor, each of whom gives a personal take on the art and craft of baseball.

Hughes, Dean. End of the Race. 1993. Atheneum, $13.95 (0-689-31779-4).

Gr. 5–7. Though both Jared, who is white, and his main competitor on the junior-high track team, African American Davin, are pressured to excel by their fathers, the two boys manage to get beyond stereotypes and like each other as people in a story in which the sports scenes are taut and physical.

Hurwitz, Johanna. Baseball Fever. 1981. illus. Morrow, $12.95 (0-688-00710-4); paper, $3.95 (0-688-10495-9).

Gr. 4–6. European-born, highly educated Mr. Feldman loathes baseball and tries to convince his 10-year-old son, Ezra, a baseball nut, to take up a nice sensible hobby, such as chess.

Jackson, Alison. Blowing Bubbles with the Enemy. 1993. Dutton, $13.99 (0-525-45056-4).

Gr. 4–6. The only girl accepted in the summer basketball program, 12-year-old

Bobbie thinks she's good enough to play on the boys' team at school; but she's not prepared for the negative reactions to her plans.

Kelly, Jim and **Carucci, Vic.** Armed and Dangerous. 1992. Doubleday, $20 (0-385-42451-5).

Gr. 9–12. In a straightforward memoir, Buffalo Bills quarterback Kelly recalls his football career—as a youth in a small Pennsylvania town, at Miami University, and as a professional player.

Korman, Gordon. The Toilet Paper Tigers. 1993. Scholastic, $13.95 (0-590-46230-X).

Gr. 4–7. According to Corey Johnson, being Little League leftovers and wearing uniforms with toilet-paper logos (team sponsor is Feather-Soft Bathroom Tissue) is bad enough without having a bossy girl managing the team, but that's the deal when the coach's pushy 12-year-old granddaughter blows into Spooner, Texas, from New York City.

Lewin, Ted. I Was a Teenage Professional Wrestler. 1993. Orchard/Richard Jackson, $16.95 (0-531-05477-2).

Gr. 7–12. With wry humor, directness, and much colorful detail, a well-known children's book illustrator recalls his boyhood fascination with wrestling and his stint as a teenage professional wrestler to pay his way through art school.

Lipsyte, Robert. The Brave. 1991. HarperCollins/Charlotte Zolotow, $15 (0-06-023915-8); paper, $3.95 (0-06-447079-2).

Gr. 7–10. The boxing scenes are outstanding in this story of teenage Indian boxer Sonny Bear, who gets in trouble when he arrives in New York City but is rescued by Manhattan cop Alfred Brooks, hero of The Contender. The sequel is The Chief (1993).

Littlefield, Bill. Champions: Stories of Ten Remarkable Athletes. 1993. illus. Little, Brown, $21.95 (0-316-52805-6).

Gr. 4–10. Profiling African American, white, and Hispanic athletes, including five women (one is disabled) from nine different sports, Littlefield focuses on their determination, dedication, and drive to reach and sustain athletic greatness.

Margolies, Jacob. Kareem Abdul-Jabbar: Basketball Great. 1992. Watts, lib. ed., $12.90 (0-531-20076-0).

Gr. 4–7. A lively profile of the man who had the longest playing career of any professional basketball star and who retired in 1989, the holder of an astonishing number of records.

Mathis, Sharon Bell. Red Dog/Blue Fly: Football Poems. 1991. illus. Viking, $13.95 (0-670-83623-0).

Gr. 3–6. Mathis traces a young boy's football season in a sensitive series of poems that captures the confusion of learning plays and signals, the frustration of incomplete passes, the pain of injury, and the warmth of comradeship.

Mills, George R. Go Big Red! The Story of a Nebraska Football Player. 1991. illus. Univ. of Illinois; dist by Johns Hopkins Univ., $19.95 (0-252-01825-7).

Gr. 9–12. Not everyone can be a Heisman winner. In a refreshing and involving memoir, a second-string player for the University of Nebraska during the mid-1970s recalls his mediocre football career and the impact college football had on his life.

Montville, Leigh. Manute: The Center of Two Worlds. 1993. Simon & Schuster, $20 (0-671-74928-5).

Gr. 8–12. Seven-foot-seven Manute Bol's cultural journey from Sudanese farmer to NBA star engagingly unfolds in a colorful biography replete with inside scoops and hoop lore.

Morris, Willie. Always Stand in against the Curve: and other Sports Stories. 1983. illus. Yoknapatawpha, Oxford, MS 38655, $15.95 (0-916242-25-0).

Gr. 9–12. The highs and lows of Morris' career as a high-school athlete form the basis of most of these autobiographical essays in which he looks back fondly at such events as Seth Morehead's unhittable curve ball, which proved to be too much for Morris' team during the 1952 Mississippi high-school baseball tournament.

Navratilova, Martina and **Vecsey, George.** Martina. 1985. Knopf, $16.95 (0-394-53640-1); Ballantine/Fawcett Crest, paper, $4.95 (0-449-20982-2).

Gr. 11–12. Up-front about her bisexuality and her career ups and downs, Navratilova's autobiography follows her life from her youth in Czechoslovakia and the difficult decision to defect through her rise to tennis stardom in the U.S.

Park, Barbara. Skinnybones. 1982. Knopf, $9.95 (0-394-93988-9); paper, $3.50 (0-394-82596).

Gr. 4–6. In a rib-tickler of a tale, Little Leaguer Alex Frankovitch (short, thin "Skinnybones"), six-year winner of the Most Improved Player Award, which he knows means going from "stink-o" to "smelly," finds himself up against his latest nemesis, T. J. Stoner, whose brother plays for the Chicago Cubs and who's so good he could be suiting up with them momentarily.

Pascarelli, Peter F. The Courage of Magic Johnson: From Boyhood Dreams to Superstar to His Toughest Challenge. 1992. Bantam, paper, $3.99 (0-553-29915-8).

Gr. 6–12. Without sugarcoating, Pascarelli recounts Johnson's life and details his impact on basketball history, conveying a sense of Johnson's record-making play and his strong, likable personality and showing how Johnson's new role as AIDS activist continues his hero image.

Puckett, Kirby. Be the Best You Can Be. 1993. illus. Waldman House, $14.95 (0-931674-20-4).

Gr. 4–6. Touching on peer pressure, on avoiding drugs and bad company, and on accepting yourself for who you are, pro baseball player Puckett, who grew up in a Chicago housing project, tells the story of his life and how he created his own future in a world that told him he didn't have one.

Slote, Alfred. The Trading Game. 1990. HarperCollins/Lippincott, $15 (0-397-32397-2); paper, $3.95 (0-06-440438-2).

Gr. 4–6. Slote grounds the moral dilemmas of growing up within the world of baseball in this story of Little Leaguer Andy Harris, who loves the game and collecting baseball cards—though the only one he really wants features his grandfather and is owned by a boy only willing to trade for the Mickey Mantle (worth $2,500) in Andy's deceased father's collection.

Soto, Gary. Taking Sides. 1991. Harcourt, paper, $6.95 (0-15-284077-X).

Gr. 6–9. When he moves from the inner-city to a middle-class suburb, Lincoln Mendoza finds he has a lot to put up with: basketball injuries, an unsympathetic coach, and misunderstandings with his old buddy and new girlfriend.

Tevis, Walter. The Queen's Gambit. 1983. Random, o.p.; Dell, paper, $8.95 (0-440-50216-0).

Gr. 8–12. Taught chess by the janitor at her orphanage, Beth Harmon develops a lifelong passion for the game and wins her first tournament at age 14, becomes American champion at 18, and goes on to play in the international circuit.

Tunis, John R. The Kid from Tomkinsville. 1990. Harcourt, $14.95 (0-15-242568-3); paper, $3.95 (0-15-242567-5).

Gr. 5–10. A reissue of a 1940 novel, this story of Roy "The Kid" Tucker who's starting his rookie year with the Brooklyn Dodgers is filled with game action as The Kid puts his knowledge of pitching to good advantage in learning to play the outfield after he suffers an arm injury.

Growing Up Is Hard to Do

Growing Up during World War II

Was it political dominance, revenge, or madness that plunged humanity into World War II? Whatever the reason, the conflagration that left millions dead and inaugurated the nuclear age has inspired both fascination and horror among novelists who still continue to explore its powerful attraction in their work. This updated bibliography of adult and teenage titles, originally compiled by Stephanie Zvirin, harks back to the anguish and drama of the war and of young people caught up in history spun out of control. While the madness of the Holocaust, an integral part of World War II fiction, underscores many of the titles assembled here, novels dealing directly with Hitler's Final Solution have been excluded. Below is a sampling of the wealth that remains, incorporating a broad range of reading and maturity levels in selections that run the gamut from contemporary classics and antiwar polemics to escapist reading that portrays war as a compelling game of glory.

Anderson, Rachel. Paper Faces. 1993. Holt, $14.95 (0-8050-2527-8).

Gr. 6–12. Preschooler Dot, who's spent her life huddled in the London slums with her mother during the Blitz, gets a chance to spend time in the country, where she finds not only food and space, but also beauty, the memories of which help her be brave when she returns to London and when her father comes back from the war, having suffered a breakdown.

Baylis-White, Mary. Sheltering Rebecca. 1991. Dutton/Lodestar, $14.95 (0-525-67349-0); Penguin/Puffin, paper, $3.99 (0-14-036448-X).

Gr. 5–8. Sixth-grader Sally Simkins befriends new student Rebecca Muller, a Jewish refugee from Nazi Germany being sheltered in Sally's English hometown, where daily life includes gas-mask drills, air raids, and makeshift bomb shelters.

Benchley, Nathaniel. Bright Candles. 1974. HarperCollins, o.p.

Gr. 6–9. Jens Hansen defies the Nazis occupying his homeland—first with youthful, unsophisticated pranks, later

within the framework of the Danish resistance.

Bermant, Chaim. Titch. 1987. St. Martin's, $13.95 (0-312-01099-0).

Gr. 10–12. Quiet, irreverent, and sexy, Bermant's story describes with wit and insight the coming-of-age of a bookworm in Manchester, England, during wartime.

Bradford, Richard. Red Sky at Morning. 1968. Lippincott, o.p.; Pocket, paper, $3.50 (0-671-50440-1); HarperCollins, paper, $6.95 (0-06-091361-4).

Gr. 9–12. When his father joins the navy and sends him and his mother to a small New Mexican town, Josh muddles along in a seriocomic fashion until his father's death forces him to take on real responsibilities.

Chang, Margaret and **Chang, Raymond.** In the Eye of War. 1990. Macmillan/Margaret K. McElderry, $14.95 (0-689-50503-5).

Gr. 5–7. An unsettling story based on Raymond Chang's boyhood experiences growing up in Shanghai during the war focuses on a boy for whom the war is mostly adventurous and sometimes inconvenient—until one day a stranger appears at the house, and the boy knows the man's presence puts his family in danger.

Degens, T. The Visit. 1982. Viking, o.p.
    Gr. 6–9. Aunt Sylvia's visit troubles Kate. Having read the diary left behind by the aunt for whom she was named, Kate knows the story of Sylvia's cruelty at a Hitler youth camp.

Ferry, Charles. Raspberry One. 1983. Houghton, $13.95 (0-395-34069-1).
    Gr. 9–12. A story of wartime friendships, loves, and tragedies—stateside and in the Pacific—evolves through the close-up perspectives of 19-year-old air crewmen Hildy and Nick.

Gallico, Paul. The Snow Goose. 1941. Knopf, $12 (0-394-44593-7).
    Gr. 7–12. Affection gradually grows between a young girl seeking aid for an injured snow goose and a hunchback artist, who helps the bird and later, with the goose circling his raft, joins the boat brigade rescuing soldiers stranded at Dunkirk.

Garfield, Brian. The Paladin. 1978. Simon & Schuster, o.p.; Bantam, paper, $3.95 (0-553-25874-5).
    Gr. 9–12. Enlisted by Churchill to do some elementary spying in Belgium, a 16-year-old schoolboy becomes a special emissary during the war.

Garrigue, Sheila. The Eternal Spring of Mr. Ito. 1985. Bradbury, $13.95 (0-02-737300-2).
    Gr. 6–9. Sara, a British evacuee to Canada, takes the part of her uncle's longtime Japanese gardener despite the anti-Japanese sentiments of others around her.

Gehrts, Barbara. Don't Say a Word. Tr. from the German by Elizabeth D. Crawford. 1986. Macmillan/Margaret K. McElderry, $13.95 (0-689-50412-8).
    Gr. 7–12. An autobiographical novel, written from the perspective of teenage Anna, tells of an anti-Nazi family living near Berlin and their mounting suffering under German tyranny.

Greene, Bette. Summer of My German Soldier. 1973. Dial, $14.95 (0-8037-8321-3); Dell, paper, $3.99 (0-440-21892-6).
    Gr. 6–9. To help a German prisoner of war escape, a 12-year-old Jewish girl defies her abusive father and the prejudiced people of her small Arkansas town.

Hahn, Mary Downing. Stepping on the Cracks. 1991. Clarion, $14.45 (0-395-58707-4); Avon/Camelot, paper, $3.99 (0-380-71900-2).
    Gr. 5–8. The popular World War II genre gains new depth in Hahn's painfully honest story about a sixth-grade girl in small-town Maryland who must decide whether to help a pacifist deserter.

Härtling, Peter. Crutches. Tr. by Elizabeth D. Crawford. 1988. Lothrop, $12.95 (0-688-07991-1).
    Gr. 6–8. Separated from his mother in the teeming crowds at a railway station as World War II is drawing to a close, Thomas is helped by a one-legged anti-Nazi war veteran called Crutches, who offers the boy food and shelter.

Haugaard, Erik. Chase Me, Catch Nobody. 1980. Houghton, o.p.
    Gr. 7–10. When a smuggler unloads a bundle of fake passports on him, a 14-year-old tourist from Denmark finds himself caught in a hide-and-seek maze with a young Jewish girl who wants to escape from Germany.

Knowles, John. A Separate Peace. 1959. Macmillan, o.p.; Bantam, paper, $3.95 (0-553-28041-4).
    Gr. 9–12. At the outbreak of the war, rivals Gene and Phineas struggle toward friendship in a New Hampshire boys' boarding school.

Kosinski, Jerzy. The Painted Bird. 1965. Houghton, o.p.; Bantam, paper, $5.99 (0-553-26520-2).

Gr. 9–12, Dark eyed and dark haired, a 10-year-old boy, separated from his parents, is labeled an outsider and abused and shunned by the Polish villagers among whom he seeks refuge.

Leffland, Ella. Rumors of Peace. 1979. HarperCollins, paper, $12 (0-06-091301-0).

Gr. 10–12. Growing up in California, a girl finds the anxieties of childhood and adolescence complicated by the turmoil of World War II America.

Levoy, Myron. Alan and Naomi. 1977. HarperCollins, paper, $3.95 (0-06-440209-6).

Gr. 7–12. A reluctant friendship evolves into one of real caring when Alan breaks through to troubled Naomi, a war refugee who struggles with memories of her father's murder by the Nazis.

Lingard, Joan. Tug of War. 1990. Dutton/Lodestar, $14.95 (0-525-67306-7); Penguin/Puffin, paper, $4.50 (0-14-036072-7).

Gr. 7–9. In the last days of the war, the Petersons, Latvian refugees who discover they cannot go home after the war ends, become separated from 14-year-old Hugo, who must make his way to Germany alone in hopes of finding his parents and twin sister.

Lowry, Lois. Number the Stars. 1989. Houghton, $13.45 (0-395-50930-0); Dell, paper, $3.99 (0-440-40327-8).

Gr. 5–7. This World War II story of two Danish girls, one Jewish, the other not, depicts the extent to which the Danes protected their Jewish countrymen from the Nazis.

Magorian, Michelle. Good Night, Mr. Tom. 1982. HarperCollins, lib. ed. $15.89 (0-06-024079-2); paper, $3.95 (0-06-440174-X).

Gr. 5–8. Badly battered and frightened,

an eight-year-old evacuee from London fills a void in the heart of a dour old man.

Matsubara, Hisako. Cranes at Dusk. 1985. Dial, o.p.

Gr. 9–12. In postwar Japan, Saya faces the pain of her defeated community as well as personal sorrow when her rigid mother, clinging to the old ways, seeks to destroy Saya's love for her freethinking father.

Mazer, Harry. The Last Mission. 1979. Delacorte, o.p.; Dell, paper, $3.50 (0-440-94797-9).

Gr. 7–12. When 15-year-old Jack Raab lies his way into the air corps and becomes a tail gunner, he never anticipates that he will be taken prisoner by the Germans.

Noonan, Michael. McKenzie's Boots. 1988. Orchard, $13.95 (0-531-05748-8).

Gr. 7–12. Australia/New Guinea is the backdrop for the tale of heroic Rod, under-age for the military, but a strapping lad who bluffs his way into service and is sent to the jungle to fight the Japanese.

Orlev, Uri. Lydia, Queen of Palestine. Tr. from the Hebrew by Hillel Halkin. 1993. Houghton, $13.90 (0-395-65669-5).

Gr. 4–6. Lydia, a feisty and sharp heroine, finds World War II a major inconvenience in a story that brilliantly captures the realities of childhood.

Orlev, Uri. The Man from the Other Side. Tr. from the Hebrew by Hillel Halkin. 1991. Houghton, $13.95 (0-395-53808-4).

Gr. 6–10. Through the maze of filthy sewers under Nazi-occupied Warsaw, teenage Marek has to help his rough Polish stepfather smuggle food and arms to the desperate Jews in the walled-up ghetto.

Pople, Maureen. The Other Side of the Family. 1988. Holt, o.p.

Gr. 9–12. Until she realizes the truth and puts aside her preconceptions and prejudices, 15-year-old Kate, evacuated from London to a small Australian town, thinks the grandmother with whom she is to live is a crotchety, uncommunicative eccentric.

Ray, Karen. To Cross a Line. 1994. Orchard/Richard Jackson, $15.95 (0-531-06831-5).

Gr. 7–10. First sentenced to pay a fine for crashing his scooter into a high-ranking Nazi's car, 17-year-old Egon Katz, a Jewish baker's apprentice, learns that the Gestapo are pursuing him and embarks on a harrowing journey to escape from Germany.

Raymond, Patrick. Daniel and Esther. 1990. Macmillan/Margaret K. McElderry, $13.95 (0-689-50504-3).

Gr. 8–12. When Daniel falls helplessly in love with Esther at their progressive English boarding school, the pair must face the agony of her return to Hitler's Austria.

Rylant, Cynthia. I Had Seen Castles. 1993. Harcourt, $10.95 (0-15-238003-5).

Gr. 6–12. John Dante looks back 50 years to when he was 18 in Pittsburgh and rushing off to fight in the war, the intensity of the home front, the urgency that made him grab at love, and the fervent desire for glory—before the loss of innocence in battle.

Sallis, Susan. A Time for Everything. 1979. HarperCollins, o.p.

Gr. 7–10. An only child, Lilly's life begins to change when her aunt and cousins arrive from bomb-torn London, and she discovers problems developing between her mother and her soldier father.

Savin, Marcia. The Moon Bridge. 1992. Scholastic, $13.95 (0-590-45873-6).

Gr. 5–7. Ruthie Fox, a fifth-grader in San Francisco in 1941, defends Japanese American Mitzi Fujimoto from schoolyard persecution and becomes her best friend; then one day Mitzi is no longer in school, having been interned in a concentration camp.

Serraillier, Ian. Escape from Warsaw. 1956. Scholastic, paper, $2.95 (0-590-43715-1).

Gr. 7–10. After their parents are sent to concentration camps, a group of young people survives together in the ruins of Nazi-occupied Warsaw.

Sevela, Ephraim. We Were Not Like Other People. Tr. by Antonina Bouis. 1989. HarperCollins, lib. ed. $14.89 (0-06-025508-0).

Gr. 8–12. Dramatic, interconnected stories of a Russian boy alone and on the run during World War II, from the Urals to Siberia and the German front, in orphanages and factories, scavenging, lying, yearning for home.

Southall, Ivan. The Long Night Watch. 1984. Farrar, $14 (0-374-34644-5).

Gr. 8–12. A young sentry fails in his duty, causing the deaths of all but a few of the refugees who wait on a South Pacific island for God to crush Hitler.

Uhlman, Fred. Reunion. 1977. Farrar, o.p.

Gr. 7–12. The close friendship between a Jewish boy and his aristocratic German classmate gradually erodes as the shadow of Hitler advances.

Vos, Ida. Hide and Seek. Tr. by Terese Edelstein and Inez Smidt. 1991. Houghton, $13.45 (0-395-56470-0).

Gr. 4–8. This autobiographical story about a young girl's experiences under the Nazi occupation is told in a series of spare vignettes that move you to image, "What if it happened to me?"

Walsh, Jill Paton. Fireweed. 1970. Farrar, o.p.

Gr. 7–10. Two teenagers find each other when they refuse to evacuate from London during the Blitz.

Watkins, Paul. Night over Day over Night. 1988. Knopf, o.p.; Avon, paper, $7.95 (0-380-70737-3).

Gr. 10–12. The battlefields are viewed from the German perspective in a bitter, unflinching portrait of a young soldier's loss of innocence.

Watkins, Yoko Kawashima. So Far from the Bamboo Grove. 1986. Lothrop, $12.95 (0-688-06110-9); Penguin/Puffin, paper, $3.99 (0-14-032385-6).

Gr. 9–12. Spoiled Yoko matures from whiny "pet" to responsible, self-reliant girl on a brutalizing journey from Korea back to her war-ravaged native Japan. In the sequel, My Brother, My Sister, and I (1994), Yoko and her older brother and sister are living as refugees in postwar Japan.

Westall, Robert. The Machine Gunners. 1976. Greenwillow, lib. ed., $13.88 (0-688-84055-8); Random, paper, $3.50 (0-679-80130-8).

Gr. 6–9. With a machine gun salvaged from a German plane gone down over Garmouth, England, Chas McGill and his friends prepare to face the enemy in a secret, homemade bomb shelter. Chas' story continues in Fathom Five.

Growing Up in the South

As with any region, when you get close, stereotype gives way to rich diversity. This retrospective bibliography, compiled by the *Booklist* Books for Youth editors, of adult and children's fiction and nonfiction is by no means all inclusive; in fact, with the exception of several "classics" that are not to be missed, the emphasis here is on newer titles. Many of the books show a contemporary South with a range of cultures and experiences—urban as well as rural. Recent accounts of the civil rights movement focus not only on the leaders, but also—like the novels—on the lives of ordinary people, on what it was like to be young at a particular time and place.

Angelou, Maya. I Know Why the Caged Bird Sings. 1970. Random, $21 (0-394-42986-9); Bantam, paper, $4.99 (0-553-27937-8).

Gr. 9–12. The first of the author's autobiographical accounts, written in lyrical prose and earthy methaphor, covers her childhood and adolescence in rural Arkansas, St. Louis, and San Francisco.

Bridgers, Sue Ellen. Permanent Connections. 1987. HarperCollins, $14 (0-06-020711-6); paper, $3.95 (0-06-447020-2).

Gr. 7–12. To help out relatives he barely knows, angry, troubled Rob is packed off to his father's North Carolina hill-country boyhood home, where Rob falls in love and finds his own peace.

Brooks, Bruce. The Moves Make the Man. 1984. HarperCollins, $15 (0-06-020679-9); paper, $3.95 (0-06-447022-9).

Gr. 7–10. Jerome, the first black to integrate a white school in his hometown, knows the moves you need to survive—in basketball and with people—but his fragile white friend, Bix, refuses to learn how to fake.

Brown, Cecil. Coming Up Down Home: Memoir of a Sharecropper's Son.

1993. Ecco; dist. by Norton, $22.95 (0-88001-293-5).

Gr. 9–12. Anger and ambivalence about his parents as well as his affection for members of the extended family among whom he lived mingle with memories of racism during the 1940s and 1950s, childhood pranks, picking cotton in the South as a child, and playing jazz in New York as an African American teen.

Brown, Dee. When the Century Was Young. 1993. August House, $23 (0-87483-273-X).

Gr. 9–12. In a simply told, engaging memoir, Brown recalls his idyllic Arkansas childhood, first job with a small Arkansas newspaper, and later work as a librarian in Washington, D.C., and Illinois.

Butterworth, William. LeRoy and the Old Man. 1980. Four Winds, o.p.; Scholastic/Point, paper, $3.25 (0-590-42711-3).

Gr. 7–12. A witness to a crime in a Chicago housing project, Leroy Chambers runs off to his grandfather in Mississippi rather than testify against gang members he's certain will kill him.

Campbell, Bebe Moore. Your Blues Ain't like Mine. 1992. Putnam, $22.95 (0-399-13746-7).

Gr. 9–12. The murder of Chicago-born Todd Armstrong, 15 and black, for not knowing his place in the segregated Mississippi of the 1950s reverberates in the lives of the white and black families involved in the killing.

Capote, Truman. The Thanksgiving Visitor. 1968. Random, $19.95 (0-394-44824-3).

Gr. 7–12. Capote's autobiographical story about Buddy, who's being raised by elderly relatives, and the spinster cousin, Miss Sook, who teaches him about compassion.

Cleaver, Vera and **Cleaver, Bill.** The Kissimmee Kid. 1981. Lothrop, $12.88 (0-688-51992-X); paper $3.95 (0-688-10975-6).

Gr. 6–8. Evelyn discovers that her brother-in-law is really a cattle rustler and must choose between lying for him and seeing him apprehended.

Covington, Dennis. Lizard. 1991. Delacorte, $15 (0-385-30307-6); Dell/Laurel-Leaf, paper, $3.50 (0-440-21490-4).

Gr. 9–12. A physcially deformed boy joins an acting company and travels the South with a man claiming to be his father. A story that makes art out of affliction and evokes images of Flannery O'Connor and Carson McCullers.

Freedom's Children: Young Civil Rights Activists Tell Their Own Stories. Ed. by Ellen Levine. 1993. illus. Putnam, $15.95 (0-399-21893-9); Avon/Flare, paper, $3.99 (0-380-72114-7).

Gr. 7–12. In this fine collection of oral histories, 30 African Americans who were children and teenagers in the 1950s and 1960s talk about what it was like for them in Alabama, Mississippi, and Arkansas: sitting in, riding at the front of the bus, integrating schools, braving arrest and violence, even death.

French, Albert. Billy. 1993. Viking, $20 (0-670-85013-6).

Gr. 9–12. A heartbreaking story of accident and racial hatred in 1930s rural Mississippi told in the plain, lyrical speech of a 10-year-old boy sentenced to die for the murder of a white girl.

Gingher, Marianne. Bobby Rex's Greatest Hit. 1988. Atheneumn, o.p.; Ballantine, paper, $3.95 (0-345-34823-0).

Gr. 9–12. In a warm, funny novel about growing up in North Carolina in the 1950s, Pally has a crush on Bobby Rex all through high school and dreams of escape from her little humdrum town.

Greene, Bette. Summer of My German Soldier. 1973. Dial, $14.95 (0-8037-8321-3); Dell, paper, $3.99 (0-440-21892-6).

Gr. 5–8. An outcast in her Arkansas hometown during World War II, 12-year-old Patty helps a prisoner of war who's shown her kindness escape, an act that teaches her to value herself.

Hall, Barbara. Dixie Storms. 1990. Harcourt, $15.95 (0-15-223825-5); Bantam, paper, $3.50 (0-553-29047-9).

Gr. 7–10. Fourteen-year-old Dutch discovers ugly secrets and grudges as well as intense love in her home, as she sees her relatives struggle with their own harshness and with the stubborn drought that threatens their Virginia farm.

Humphreys, Josephine. Rich in Love. 1987. Viking, o.p.; Penguin, paper, $10 (0-14-017432-X).

Gr. 9–12. Firmly rooted in her South Carolina home, 17-year-old Lucille remains a strong center for her troubled parents and beautiful, pregnant older sister, as Lucille herself finds passion and self-acceptance.

Lee, Harper. To Kill a Mockingbird. 1961. HarperCollins/Lippincott, o.p.; Warner, paper, $4.99 (0-446-31078-6).

Gr. 9–12. Eight-year-old Scout describes growing up in a small Alabama town where her father's courageous defense of a black man falsely accused of rape exposes the racism in the community and brings violence into her naive, childhood world.

Marino, Jan. The Day That Elvis Came to Town. 1991. Little, Brown, $15.95 (0-316-54618-6); Avon/Camelot, paper, $3.50 (0-380-71672-0).

Gr. 7–10. Set in the South in the early 1960s, this brings together a teenager named Wanda, who spends most of her time in her bedroom listening to Elvis records, and a jazz-singer/boarder, who claims she knows the singer.

McCullers, Carson. The Member of the Wedding. 1946. Houghton, o.p.; Bantam, paper, $4.50 (0-553-25051-5).

Gr. 8–12. Originally published as a novel, which McCullers turned into a play, this story set during a summer in the Deep South, centers on lonely 12-year-old Frankie Addams, who is crushed when her beloved brother, a recently returned soldier, doesn't take her on his honeymoon.

Moore, Yvette. Freedom Songs. 1991. Orchard, $14.95 (0-531-05812-3).

Gr. 6–12. New York teenager Sheryl loves visiting her family in rural North Carolina, but in 1963 she faces the Jim Crow reality of her cousins' daily segregation. Then her young Uncle Pete's life is endangered when he joins the freedom riders.

Naylor, Phyllis R. Night Cry. 1984. Atheneum, $13.95 (0-689-31017-X).

Gr. 4–6. Left alone at their cabin in the backwoods Mississippi hill country when her father takes a job as a traveling salesman, 13-year-old Ellen Stump not only comes to terms with her fears, but also saves a terrified child from a kidnapper.

Newton, Suzanne. I Will Call It Georgie's Blues. 1983. Viking, o.p.; Penguin/Puffin, $3.95 (0-14-034536-1).

Gr. 7–10. The town minister bullies his family. Fifteen-year-old Neal has a secret escape in his music from the rage and pain

of his home—but his fragile little brother is breaking down.

Oates, Stephen B. Let the Trumpet Sound: The Life of Martin Luther King, Jr. 1982. HarperCollins, o.p.; NAL/Plume, paper, $5.99 (0-451-62350-9).

Gr. 8–12. One of the many fine biographies of the great civil rights leader, Martin Luther King, Jr., who became a national symbol of freedom and justice.

Parks, Rosa and **Haskins, Jim.** Rosa Parks: My Story. 1992. Dial, $17 (0-8037-0673-1).

Gr. 6–10. A straightforward, uncompromising autobiography of the civil rights leader, told with the kind of unflinching honesty and dignity embodied by Parks.

Perera, Hilda. Kiki: A Cuban Boy's Adventures in America. 1992. Pickering Press, P.O. Box 331531, Miami, Fl 33233, paper, $12.95 (0-940495-24-4).

Gr. 4–8. This funny, poignant novel about a Cuban immigrant boy in Miami in the 1960s is candid about the conflicts of a young person caught between two cultures.

Rylant, Cynthia. A Fine White Dust. 1986. Bradbury, $13.95 (0-02-777240-3); Dell, paper, $3.50 (0-440-42499-2).

Gr. 6–8. Thirteen-year-old Pete is struck by the charisma of an itinerant reverend, but Preacher Man takes the boy's dreams with him when he leaves the small North Carolina town.

Sanders, Dori. Clover. 1990. Algonquin, $13.95 (0-945575-26-2).

In a story set in the modern small-town South, 10-year-old Clover tells how she and her new white stepmother try to make a life together while they struggle with their grief and difference.

Stolz, Mary. Stealing Home. 1992. HarperCollins, $14 (0-06-021154-7).

Gr. 4–6. Cozy is one of Thomas' favorite words, and it perfectly describes the warm,

Growing Up Is Hard to Do

messy home he's always had with his grandfather and his cat, Ringo, near the Florida shore. Then Great-aunt Linzy moves in and tries to clean up all their clutter.

Stone, Bruce. Half Nelson, Full Nelson. 1985. HarperCollins, paper, $2.95 (0-06-447047-4).

Gr. 7–10. In a funny novel about real and fake togetherness, 16-year-old Nelson loves his family, and he's trying to keep them together in a tacky Florida trailer park. His 270-pound father dreams of making it in big-time wrestling, but his wife wants a "civilized" life.

Straight, Susan. I Been in Sorrow's Kitchen and Licked Out All the Pots. 1992. Hyperion; dist. by Little, Brown, $19.95 (1-56282-963-7).

Gr. 9–12. When her mother dies, 15-year-old Marietta—tall, strong, and reticent—takes off for Charleston, where she works until, pregnant, she goes home to her tiny, nurturing North Carolina coastal community to have her twin boys, and later sees them make good as football stars.

Taylor, Mildred. Let the Circle Be Unbroken. 1981. Dial, $15.95 (0-8037-4748-9); Penguin/Puffin, paper, $3.99 (0-14-034893-1).

Gr. 6–9. An absorbing and instructive exploration of the southern black experience in the 1930s features the Logan family in this, the third saga in their story.

Walker, Alice. The Color Purple. 1982. Harcourt, $15.95 (0-15-119153-0); Pocket, paper, $5.99 (0-671-72779-6).

Gr. 10–12. Sisters Nettie and Celie are separated as young girls—Celie to become the child bride of a widower, and Nettie to be taken by a black family to Africa as a missionary; sustained in her harsh and poverty-stricken marriage only by a series of trusting letters she addresses to God and her sister, Celie eventually meets a woman with whom she can find love and security and is blessed again when Nettie returns after a 30-year absence.

Walter, Mildred Pitts. Mississippi Challenge. 1992. Bradbury, $18.95 (0-02-792301-0).

Gr. 7–12. This in-depth history of the civil rights struggle in one state tells how ordinary people worked and protested and suffered to change the political system. The sometimes complicated legal struggle of the 1960s is set side by side with personal testimony.

Webb, Sheyann and **Nelson, Rachel W.** Selma, Lord, Selma: Girlhood Memories of the Civil-Rights Days. 1980. Univ. of Alabama, $14.95 (0-8173-0031-7).

Gr. 7–12. Rachel and Sheyann remember themselves at age eight in those days of tension in Selma: marching, singing, demonstrating, being set upon by troopers, going to meetings, and talking about those who had been jailed or beaten or killed.

White, Ruth. Weeping Willow. 1992. Farrar, $16 (0-374-38255-7).

Gr. 7–10. Though she's raped by her stepfather, Tiny survives and becomes strong in a convincing novel about friendships, first love, loss, and tragedy.

Wilkinson, Brenda. Ludell. 1975. HarperCollins, lib. ed., $14.89 (0-06-026492-6); paper, $3.95 (0-06-440419-6).

Gr. 6–8. Ludell is a bouncy, saucy 11-year-old growing up within a loving black family in Waycross, Georgia, around 1955 in this first book of a lively series that takes Ludell from childhood to adulthood.

Wright, Richard. Black Boy. 1945. HarperCollins, paper, $6 (0-06-081250-8).

Gr. 7–12. This classic autobiography by one of the great naturalistic American writers is dramatic, intense, and immediate, and it includes searing scenes of confrontation. Wright is forced to mask his pride in himself, yet he refuses to let the white South break his spirit.

Growing Up in the South

Growing Up in the Southwest

It's not all desert. Mountains and ski resorts, metroplexes and malls, lakes, rivers, and the coastline of Texas, all have their place as part of the landscape of the Southwest. Just as diverse are the people. Some with roots in ancient civilizations, others arriving only yesterday. As multifaceted as its diverse communities, the literature of the Southwest reveals the coexistence of many languages, cultures, traditions, and beliefs.

The titles selected by Karen Ferris Morgan, a storyteller and doctoral student at the School of Library and Information Studies at Texas Woman's University, Denton, for this bibliography represent the old and the new, voices of mainstream and minority groups. Concentrated flavors of the Southwest may be part of these books, but they stress universal themes and give us a deeper understanding of America.

Anaya, Rudolfo A. Bless Me, Ultima. 1972. Tonatiuh-Quinto Sol International, paper, $14.95 (0-89229-002-1).

Gr. 7–12. Antonio Juan Mares y Luna narrates this powerful novel about the special relationship he has with Ultima, a curandera, who comes to live with his family the summer he turns seven.

Ashabranner, Brent. Photos. by **Conklin, Paul.** Dark Harvest: Migrant Farmworkers in America. 1985. illus. Dodd, Mead, o.p.; Shoestring/Linnet, $16.50 (0-208-02391-7).

Gr. 5–12. Ashabranner gives a voice to a people who remain invisible to the majority of Americans. Conklin's black-and-white photographs reveal their faces. Also recommended are *The Vanishing Border* and *Born to the Land*, about other aspects of the Southwest.

Axelrod, Alan. Songs of the Wild West. 1991. illus. Simon & Schuster, $19.95 (0-671-74775-4).

Gr. 4–12. Forty-five songs, with musical arrangements by Dan Fox, are accompanied by intriguing background information and illustrations, such as "An Arizona Cowboy" by Remington and artifacts that include a Topps Chewing Gum card of Billy the Kid.

Bess, Clayton. Tracks. 1986. Houghton, o.p.

Gr. 7–12. Riding the rails in Texas and Oklahoma during the Depression, Blue and his older brother travel with hoboes, get caught in dusters, and witness the Ku Klux Klan mutilate a young Mexican.

Blume, Judy. Tiger Eyes. 1981. Bradbury, $14.95 (0-02-711080-X); Dell, paper, $3.99 (0-440-98469-6).

Gr. 7–10. Staying with relatives in New Mexico after her dad's brutal murder, 15-year-old Davey must deal with her mom's depression, her own grief, and the fears she senses in some of the people in Los Alamos. As she climbs nearby canyons and meets college-age Wolf, Davey grows and changes.

Bonner, Cindy. Lily: A Love Story. 1992. Algonquin, $17.95 (0-945575-95-5).

Gr. 9–12. In Texas in the 1880s, two young men take an interest in 15-year-old Lily. One is the college-bound son of a respectable ranching family, but it is the other, the youngest member of a notorious outlaw gang, whom Lily comes to love.

Bradford, Richard. Red Sky at Morning. 1968. HarperCollins/Lippincott, paper, $11 (0-06-091361-4).

Gr. 8–12. Seventeen-year-old Josh Arnold and his mother leave Alabama to live in a remote New Mexico town while his father fights in World War II. As his mother drinks and plays bridge, Josh learns some Spanish and comments with honesty and a dry sense of humor about social class, prejudice, skin color, sex, and friendship.

Cannon, A. E. The Shadow Brothers. 1990. Delacorte, o.p.; Dell, paper, $3.50 (0-440-21167-0).

Gr. 7–12. Navajo Henry Yazzie, who lives off the reservation with a foster family, finds his life changed by a Hopi teenage boy who transfers into school, a white girlfriend (who may be using Henry to get attention from her father), and the shooting of Henry's father. Told with humor, affection, and occasional bewilderment by Henry's foster brother, Marcus.

Cisneros, Sandra. Woman Hollering Creek and Other Stories. 1991. Random, $17.50 (0-394-57654-3); Vintage, paper, $10 (0-679-73856-8).

Gr. 9–12. Whether writing about playing with Barbies (one with mean eyes and a ponytail, the other with bubble hair) or loving Flavio, former shrimper, field worker, and exterminator ("Always gonna be bugs"), Cisneros writes stories that can be funny, moving, and insightful.

DeVito, Cara. Where I Want to Be. 1993. Houghton, $13.95 (0-395-64592-1).

Gr. 7–12. Life in rural Arizona is far from uneventful and includes bus accidents, dates who get drunk, and armed robbery in this story told from the perspective of bright, rebellious, 15-year-old Kristie, abandoned by her mother and raised by her step-brothers after the death of her father.

Dobie, J. Frank. I'll Tell You a Tale: An Anthology. 1960. Little, Brown, o.p.; Univ. of Texas, paper $12.95 (0-292-73821-8).

Gr. 7 and up. Calling himself not a folklorist simply recording the tales he hears, but a writer who takes tales from other sources and polishes them, Dobie offers the flavor of older Southwest storytelling in this anthology.

Duncan, Lois. Killing Mr. Griffin. 1978. Little, Brown, $15.95 (0-316-19549-9); Dell, paper, $3.99 (0-440-94515-1).

Gr. 8–12. With uncomfortable and disturbing realism, the idea of killing high-school English teacher Mr. Griffin becomes a reality. The action takes place in and around New Mexico's Sandia Mountains, as several teens decide whether they'll follow a dangerous classmate or take responsibility for their actions.

Fernandez, Roberta. Intaglio: A Novel in Six Stories. 1990. Arte Publico, paper, $9.50 (1-55885-016-3).

Gr. 9–12. A collection of images about six strong women of the Southwest as seen through the eyes of a young female narrator. From the dressmaker who specializes in transformations, to the caregiver for whom Dia de los Muertos has such special significance, Fernandez enables readers to become immersed in her characters.

Freedman, Russell. Cowboys of the Wild West. 1985. Clarion, $14.95 (0-89919-301-3); paper, $5.70 (0-395-54800-4).

Gr. 4–9. With archival photographs, a map, drawings, and parts of songs, Freedman gives an accurate picture of cowboy life, while dispelling some of the myths found in movies.

Greenberg, Joanne. Simple Gifts. 1986. Holt, paper, $7.95 (0-8050-0540-4).

Gr. 8–12. Every family has its secrets, but the Fleuris aren't just any family. They are selected to play the part of 1880 Colorado pioneers for tourists who want an "authentic" western experience, and family secrets are humorously revealed through the voices of various characters.

Hillerman, Tony. The Boy Who Made Dragonfly: A Zuni Myth. 1986. Univ. of New Mexico, paper, $8.95 (0-8263-0910-0).

Gr. 4 and up. Well known for his mysteries set in the Southwest, Hillerman here retells an old Zuni myth. Gently crafted in the style of oral tradition, the tale raises questions about a society's abandonment of the young and the old and the wasting of resources.

Hinton, S. E. The Outsiders. 1967. Viking, $13 (0-670-53257-6); Dell, paper, $3.99 (0-440-96769-4).
Gr. 7–12. Streetwise, 14, and orphaned, Ponyboy is part of a close-knit gang, but he also loves movies, books, and his two older brothers.

Hobbs, Will. Downriver. 1991. Atheneum, $14.95 (0-689-31690-9); Bantam, paper, $3.50 (0-553-29717-1).
Gr. 7–12. Eight teen misfits, half male, half female, explore the Grand Canyon and learn more than just how to ride the waters of the Colorado River, as they leave adult supervision behind.

Hogan, Linda. Mean Spirit. 1990. Atheneum, $19.95 (0-689-12101-6); Ivy, paper, $4.99 (0-8041-0863-3).
Hogan, a Chickasaw poet, essayist, and author, has combined historical fact and fiction to create an intensely powerful book about Oklahoma oil, profit, loss, traditions, people, pride, and survival.

Koertge, Ron. The Arizona Kid. 1988. Little, Brown/Joy Street, $14.95 (0-316-50101-8); Avon/Flare, paper, $3.50 (0-380-70776-4).
Gr. 8–12. With natural humor, Billy tells the story of his experiences working at a racetrack in Tucson, Arizona, during the summer he spends getting to know and feel comfortable with his gay uncle.

Martinez, Max. Schoolland. 1988. Arte Publico, paper, $9.50 (0-934770-87-5).
Gr. 9–12. In rough, honest language, the teen narrator describes his grandfather, the rest of his large Mexican American family, and their life in a small Texas town in a period of drought in the 1950s.

Mazzio, Joann. Leaving Eldorado. 1993. Houghton, $13.95 (0-395-64381-3).

Gr. 7–10. Writing letters addressed to her mother who recently died, Maude reveals her struggles, initially, to make it on her own in a New Mexican mining town and, later, to leave and take charge of her life. Mazzio's The One Who Came Back is a story of friendship and death involving two teens—one Mexican American, the other Anglo.

Mikaelson, Ben. Sparrow Hawk Red. 1993. Hyperion; dist. by Little, Brown, $14.95 (1-56282-387-6).
Gr. 4–8. His dad thinks Ricky's mature enough to fly solo but not old enough to know all the facts surrounding his mother's murder by drug smugglers; however, Ricky goes to Mexico posing as a homeless street kid to take revenge on the drug cartel and, in the process, comes to understand the importance of his heritage.

Momaday, N. Scott. House Made of Dawn. 1968. HarperCollins, paper, $11 (0-06-091633-8).
Gr. 10–12. A Pulitzer Prize–winning author and poet, Momaday writes about Abel, who tries to find his way in two conflicting worlds. In The Way to Rainy Mountain, Momaday retells myths of his people, the Kiowas, and relates them to history and his own childhood.

Myers, Walter Dean. The Righteous Revenge of Artemis Bonner. 1992. HarperCollins, $14 (0-06-020844-9).
Gr. 5–9. Tongue-in-cheek humor, slapstick, and melodrama team with action as 15-year-old Artemis hunts Catfish Grimes and Lucy Featherdip to avenge the death of his uncle Ugly Ned and regain Ned's treasure.

Page, Suzanne. A Celebration of Being. 1989. illus. Northland, paper, $19.95 (0-87358-495-3).
Gr. 5–12. Page's photographs and text help readers visualize the people, both Navajo and Hopi—two tribes, two cultures—and the variety of contemporary life in the high country of the Southwest.

Growing Up Is Hard to Do

Growing Up Listening

Although identical in content to their print counterparts, unabridged audiobooks are, nevertheless, a different format. As discussed in "Voice-over: Where Have All the Readers Gone?" [BKL Mr 15 93], audiobooks can introduce nonreaders to literary works; they can expand the narrative far beyond the printed page; and they have unique properties that affect the selection process and the literary experience. The most critical factor is the narrator, who interprets the text for listeners. Not only is the reader able to employ distinctive voices for the various characters, but a top-notch narrator can also suggest personality, age, era, ethnicity, mood, and intent through tone, emphasis, phrasing, accent, stress, and various other effects. George Guidall, for example, becomes a child, a monk, and a warrior of feudal Japan in *The Boy and the Samurai*; a New York teenager in *The Last Mission*; and a Jewish concentration camp survivor in *Dawn*; in doing so, the reader reveals important elements of the text to adolescent listeners. The following list of audiobooks, compiled by Karen Harris, is a sampling of the treats awaiting teenage readers/listeners.

Adrift. By Steven Callahan. Read by Dick Estell. Books on Tape. 9hr. 6 cassettes, $48.

Gr. 9–12. Callahan recounts the 75 agonizing days he spent alone and adrift in a five-foot raft until, after having traveled some 1,800 miles, he was finally rescued.

The Boy and the Samurai. By Erik Christian Haugaard. Read by George Guidall. Recorded Books. 7hr. 5 cassettes, $39.

Gr. 7–8. Orphaned, six-year-old Saru must live by his wits as war, hunger, and privation make survival increasingly unlikely. This flawless reading magically evokes the world of feudal Japan.

A Charmed Life. By Diana Wynne Jones. Read by Tony Robinson. Chivers. 5hr. 4 cassettes, $29.95.

Gr. 7–8. Robinson's English-accented reading helps set the tone for this witty tale of witchcraft and hubris.

The Chocolate War. By Robert Cormier. Read by George Guidall. Recorded Books. 6hr. 5 cassettes, $39.

Gr. 9–12. Multiple levels of Cormier's gripping story of corruption and evil in a boys' school are revealed in this highly skilled reading.

Dawn. By Elie Wiesel. Read by George Guidall. Recorded Books. 3hr. 2 cassettes, $18.

Gr. 10–12. Wiesel's account of a concentration camp survivor who must make a desperate moral decision is told with a tension that is all but unbearable.

A Day No Pigs Would Die. By Robert Newton Peck. Read by Robert Sevra. Listening Library. 3hr. 3 cassettes, $22.98.

Gr. 7–8. Sevra's clear, straightforward reading allows the natural rhythms of Peck's superlative narrative to emerge with tremendous power.

81 Famous Poems. Read by Alexander Scourby and others. Audio Partners. 2hr. 2 cassettes, $15.95.

Gr. 9–12. Students will be helped immeasurably in comprehension of these familiar classic works, taken from *The Norton Anthology of Poetry,* when they hear each poem clearly articulated and properly scanned.

Ernest Hemingway: Short Stories by Ernest Hemingway. Read by Alexander Scourby. Listening Library. 2hr. 2 cassettes, $16.95.

Gr. 9–12. "The Short Happy Life of Francis Macomber" and "The Snows of Kilimanjaro," narrated by the dean of audiobook readers, make a perfect introduction to the works of Hemingway.

Eva. By Peter Dickinson. Read by Jill Tanner. Recorded Books. 8hr. 6 cassettes, $42.

Gr. 8–10. Irreparably damaged in an accident, Eva now inhabits the body of a chimp. This accommodation precipitates events that horrify her parents and plunge Eva into a series of complex moral dilemmas.

Granny Was a Buffer Girl. By Berlie Doherty. Read by the author. G. K. Hall. 4 hr. 3 cassettes, $26.95.

Gr. 8–10. As Jess gets ready to leave home, she recalls her family history in this warm and charming novel, read here by the author.

Hatchet. By Gary Paulsen. Read by Peter Coyote. Bantam Audio. 3hr. 3 cassettes, $17.95.

Gr. 8–12. Peter Coyote offers an appropriate blend of ruggedness and sensitivity in his reading of Paulson's popular survival story.

Homecoming. By Cynthia Voigt. Read by Barbara Caruso. Recorded Books. 14hr. 10 cassettes, $75.

Gr. 7–8. Dicey's adventures begin in this novel, which recounts the abandonment of the Tillerman children and their eventual arrival at a safe haven with their grandmother.

I Am the Cheese. By Robert Cormier. Read by Jeff Woodman and John R. Jones. Recorded Books. 5hr. 4 cassettes, $32.

Gr. 8–12. This intellectually demanding, existential novel is rendered considerably more accessible by Woodman's and Jones' excellent interpretations.

I Can Hear the Mourning Dove. By James Bennett. Read by Barbara Rosenblatt. Recorded Books. 7hr. 5 cassettes, $39.

Gr. 9–12. Unable to cope with her grief after her father's death and victimized by the violence in her community, Grace is institutionalized. Luke, a frustrated and angry resident, helps her learn to live with loss, face her anxieties, and regain some control over her life.

Julie of the Wolves. By Jean Craighead George. Read by Christina Moore. Recorded Books. 4hr. 3 cassettes, $23.

Gr. 7–9. Moore's stirring reading transports listeners to the frozen tundra where Julie/Miyax, caught between cultures in a rapidly changing world, searches for her true identity.

The Last Mission. By Harry Mazer. Read by George Guidall. Recorded Books. 5hr. 4 cassettes, $32.

Gr. 8–10. Jack Raab lies about his age so that he can fight in World War II. His dreams of glory are shattered by the carnage he sees and the terror he experiences, as he learns the difference between his naive vision and war's reality.

Lord of the Flies. By William Golding. Read by the author. Listening Library. 7hr. 6 cassettes, $44.98.

Gr. 9–12. Although Golding lacks the skills of a professional actor, the loss is more than made up for by his commentary at the beginning and between chapters, which provides insight into his writing process.

Growing Up Is Hard to Do

Lyddie. By Katherine Paterson. Read by Alyssa Bresnahan. Recorded Books. 7hr. 5 cassettes, $39.

Gr. 7–9. A model of historical fiction, *Lyddie* offers some fascinating glimpses into the life of "mill girls" in New England during the Industrial Revolution.

M. C. Higgins, the Great. By Virginia Hamilton. Read by Roscoe Lee Browne. Recorded Books. 8hr. 6 cassettes, $42.

Gr. 7–9. Browne's reading, perfectly matched to Hamilton's text, vividly re-creates M. C.'s view from atop Sarah's mountain.

Narrative of the Life of Frederick Douglass. By Frederick Douglass. Read by Charles Turner. Recorded Books 4hr. 3 cassettes, $23.

Gr. 9–12. Turner's flawless reading of this most heart-wrenching indictment of slavery offers an unforgettable experience.

Old Yeller. By Fred Gipson. Read by Wolfram Kandinsky. Books on Tape. 5 hr. 5 cassettes, $30.

Gr. 7–9. This timeless young adult classic, set in Texas in the mid-1900s, concerns the coming-of-age of Travis who, with the help of an extraordinary dog, faces the brutal challenges of survival in frontier America.

The Outsiders. By S. E. Hinton. Read by Spike McClure. Recorded Books. 6hr. 4 cassettes, $32.

Gr. 8–10. McClure is perfectly cast as Ponyboy in Hinton's enduringly popular novel of adolescents unwanted and un-protected by an indifferent society.

The Perilous Gard. By Elizabeth Marie Pope. Read by Jill Tanner. Recorded Books. 9hr. 7 cassettes, $52.

Gr. 8–10. A mystical historical romance for the hopelessly romantic, this Newbery Honor Book is given an impeccable inter-pretation by Tanner.

To Kill a Mockingbird. By Harper Lee. Read by Sally Darling. Recorded Books. 13hr. 9 cassettes, $68.

Gr. 7–10. This staple of many reading programs is performed here to perfection as Darling allows the drama of Lee's words to build to an unforgettable climax.

A Wizard of Earthsea. By Ursula K. LeGuin. Read by Rob Inglis. Recorded Books. 7hr. 5 cassettes, $39.

Gr. 7–10. In this first work in the Earthsea trilogy, Inglis effortlessly conjures up the magical world beloved by LeGuin fans.

A Wrinkle in Time. By Madeleine L'Engle. Read by the author. Listening Library 6hr. 4 cassettes, $32.98.

Gr. 7–9. L'Engle introduces her New-bery award novel briefly and then reads it with an enthusiasm that lends a special, personal touch to the narrative.

Distributors

Audio Partners, 1133 High St., Auburn, CA 95603. 915-888-7803.

Bantam Audio Publishing, Education and Library Div., 666 Fifth Ave., New York, NY 10103. 212-782-9523.

Books on Tape, P. O. Box 7900, Newport Beach, CA 92658. 800-525-6657

Chivers Audio Books. 1 Lafayette Rd., Box 1450, Hampton, NH 03842-0015. 800-621-0182.

G. K. Hall Audio Books, Order Dept., 100 Front St., Box 500, Riverside, NJ 08075. 207-948-2962.

Listening Library,1 Park Ave., Old Green-wich, CT 06870

Recorded Books Library Service, 270 Skip-jack Rd., Prince Frederick, MD 20678. 800-638-1304.

Author Index

Growing Up Is Hard to Do

Title Index

Growing Up Is Hard to Do

Growing Up Is Hard to Do